CHINESE
ARCHITECTURE

Discovering China

CHINESE
ARCHITECTURE

WANG QIJUN

Better Link Press

This book is edited and designed by the Editorial Committee of *Cultural China* series

Managing Directors: Wang Youbu, Xu Naiqing
Editorial Director: Wu Ying
Editors: Yang Xiaohe, Kirstin Mattson

Text, Illustrations and Photographs: Wang Qijun
Translation of Caption and Overview of Terms: Cao Jianxin

Cover Design: Wang Wei
Interior Design: Yuan Yinchang, Li Jing, Hu Bin

ISBN: 978-1-60220-118-7

Address any comments about *Discovering China: Chinese Architecture* to:

Better Link Press
99 Park Ave
New York, NY 10016
USA

or

Shanghai Press and Publishing Development Company
F 7 Donghu Road, Shanghai, China (200031)
Email: comments_betterlinkpress@hotmail.com

Computer typeset by Yuan Yinchang Design Studio, Shanghai
Printed in China by Shenzhen Donnelley Printing Co., Ltd.

1   3   5   7   9   10   8   6   4   2

CONTENTS

CONTENTS

CONTENTS

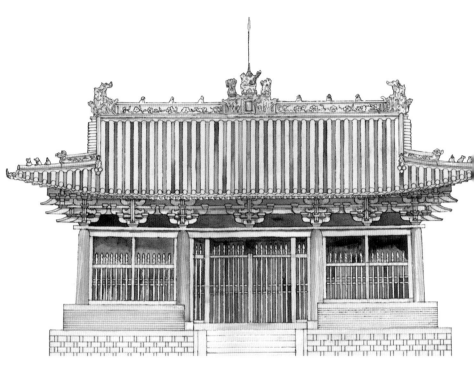

This temple in Taiyuan, Shanxi Province, has features that are typical of palaces of the Song dynasty.

FUNDAMENTAL FEATURES OF ANCIENT CHINESE ARCHITECTURE

Ancient Chinese architecture is notable not only for its technical and artistic achievement, but also for what it can tell us about traditional Chinese culture. Through the ages, the buildings of China represent the aspirations of its rulers, upheaval and change due to war and dynastic succession, and developments in religious and social thought, as well as migration and geographic factors.

The remarkable artistic and structural principles of the architecture of ancient China rank it as one of the world's great systems of ancient architecture, along with that of Egypt, the Tigris and Euphrates region, India, the Americas, the Islamic world and Europe. Along with only ancient Islamic, Chinese and European architecture, it has endured to remain influential to the present day. It also strongly influenced its neighbors, particularly Korea and Japan. Therefore, ancient Chinese architecture is a truly a precious heritage of world civilization.

Ancient Chinese architecture presents a wide diversity of features, reflecting different historical stages as well as strong regional characteristics. The field of ancient Chinese architecture covers an extraordinary range of structures, including entire cities (urban planning); palaces and royal mausoleums; Buddhist, Taoist and Confucian temples and other religious buildings; and government offices and institutions of higher learning. It also includes folk architecture, such as residential dwellings, stockaded village complexes, family altars, and opera platforms. In addition, garden design plays a much more important role in ancient Chinese architecture than in other architectural traditions.

Works of architecture have much to tell us about the time in which they were created. For example, take the façade of a palace hall from the

peak of the Song dynasty (960 – 1279). Its columns incline slightly inward, giving the feeling of slender apex rising from a large base. The horizontal supports (purlins) in the eaves of the side bays elevate upward slightly at the end toward the building's outer edges. Therefore, eaves are not a continuous horizontal line, but rather curve upward, similar to a crescent. The roof has a two-slope form with concave curves, rather than the two equal sides of an isosceles triangle, with the curvature dependent on precise technical calculations. It is clear that the design of this building is both elegant and complicated. This is not surprising considering the Song dynasty was a time of cultural brilliance, radical growth in urban life, and economic and industrial development.

In addition to historical and social context, the architecture of ancient China strongly relates to the arts and culture of China. Over its

This drawing shows a typical elevation of a Song dynasty building. The purlins under the eaves are horizontal only in the central bay, while the traverse purlins of the side bays rise gradually toward the outer edge. The tops of the columns incline inward, while the lower sections incline outward, thus having a slight triangular appearance.

development, Chinese art has differed in many fundamental ways from Western art. Western art typically values capturing the real, for instance, the anatomical preciseness of the human figure or the use of naturalistic colors. Chinese paintings emphasize the ideal, using lines rather than light and shade, and focusing on free strokes and artistic expression rather than capturing detail. The Chinese concept of the body is also quite different. For example, in order to describe a general, Western art might emphasize the four strong limbs while the Chinese emphasize the robust body, such as when creating the guardian general sculptures in a temple. This expressive approach informs ancient Chinese architecture, setting it apart from other architectural systems in the world.

The color scheme of ancient Chinese buildings is also unique, using colors not found in other architectural traditions, and applying them in

Seen from a side elevation, the roofs of Song dynasty buildings are triangular with two curves. The curves incline sharply at the ridges but soon flatten out.

unusual ways. For example, roofs are decorated with golden, green, blue, brown and black glaze. Glazed tiles of different colors may be put together to form a decorative pattern on some roofs. For some buildings, a different principal color is used on the roof of each floor, creating a complex design.

Doors and window frames are also a major part of the color scheme. Since classical Chinese architecture features a wood frame structure that is load-bearing, doors and windows can occupy a large area, and therefore their coloration adds greatly to the overall design. Intensely-colored walls were yet another way to add color to architecture. The Forbidden City is an iconic example of this attention to color. Its red walls and yellow tiles shining under the blue sky were intended to evoke magnificence, prosperity and fortune. Such color saturation is rarely seen in ancient architecture of other areas.

In addition to using color on architectural elements, Chinese architecture

Zhihuihai, located at Longevity Hill of the Summer Palace in Beijing, is gorgeously-colored, with a glazed outer wall. This shows its southern elevation.

often incorporates actual decorative paintings. The most important are those that appear under the eaves and on the upper ends of the walls. While some are composed of geometrical patterns, they also include thematic or figurative pictures, sometimes representing legends or historical events.

Although the decorative paintings were in bright colors, their location under the eaves or in interiors meant that they were in the shadow. As a result, the main colors of classical Chinese architecture are those of the roofs and walls. However, due to the durability of architecture,

The Summer Palace in Beijing consists of many small gardens. This is a colored painting depicting "farming and weaving" on the long corridor.

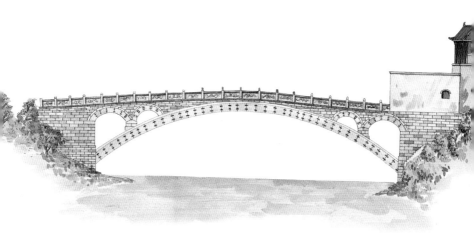

Anji Bridge (Zhaozhou Bridge), in Zhaoxian County of Hebei Province, was built in the Sui dynasty. It is the longest among the world's early single-span, open-shoulder stone arch bridges.

buildings often provide rare examples of painting from early dynasties, which have not lasted in other media.

While the arts influenced many forms of ancient Chinese architecture, perhaps the clearest influence can be seen in garden design. Many gardens are designed to evoke Chinese landscape paintings, whether in theme, color scheme or layout. Influences from music, literature and poetry are also prominent in Chinese gardens.

As one would expect, great attention was given to the aesthetic and functional features of the palaces of emperors and the homes of the wealthy. However, ancient Chinese architecture covers a full range, and many craftsmen attached importance to the structure, function, design and decoration of all buildings. They even tried to avoid dullness and exercised their imagination for everyday buildings such as stores, workshops and residences.

Attention to material is a hallmark of classical Chinese architecture, and the use of different materials in varied ways demonstrates developed and innovative technical skills. In the Han dynasty (206 BC – AD 220), stone was used to build complicated arches and domes—all the more remarkable because they were in the underground buildings in royal tombs, where they would be seen by very few. Anji Bridge (Zhaozhou Bridge) in

Copy by the author of *The Landscape Scroll*. The original piece by Song dynasty artist Gao Keming is now preserved in The Metropolitam Museum of Art in USA.

Hebei Province, built during the time of Kaihuang reign and Daye reign (581 – 618) of the Sui dynasty, had the longest span of any single-arch, open-shoulder stone bridge in the world at that time.

Stone, however, was not a typical medium for building houses. The Yangtze River and the Yellow River are "Mother Rivers" for the Chinese nation, and their ancestors used to live in this region. Some dwelled first in natural caves, then modified cliff caves and then excavated caves to form earthwork houses. Other used tree branches to construct nest buildings, and then put up tents. Their descendants inherited the architectural traditions of using earth and wood. Therefore, the construction of ancient Chinese architecture is also called "work of earth and wood." Although later on, the Chinese mastered new construction materials such as stones, tiles and colored glaze, earth and wood was still the traditional and favorite construction material.

Today, of course, steel and glass are widely used in modern buildings, and the traditional construction of classical Chinese architecture is rarely used. However, Chinese architectural art is an important part of the world's cultural heritage, and an understanding of it can lead to a greater understanding of China itself.

OVERVIEW OF TERMS

Types of Buildings

English	Chinese	Chinese Pinyin	Image
Buddhist buildings in the Han style	汉式佛教建筑	hanshi fojiao jianzhu	
Buddhist buildings in the Tibetan style	藏式佛教建筑	zangshi fojiao jianzhu	
Cave dwellings	窑洞民居	yaodong minju	

Description

The layout of the earliest Han Buddhist buildings were modeled on those in India, without halls but with pagodas for holding Buddhist bone remains. In the Tang and Song dynasties (618 – 1279), Buddhist temples developed into a courtyard pattern, with halls as a chief feature. A complete Buddhist temple generally consists of seven halls that have specific purposes. After the Ming dynasty (1368 – 1644), this seven hall system took a basic fixed form, with variations according to sect or branch. Taking Zen as an example, the seven halls are the entrance, Hall of Buddha, dharma hall, monk hall, kitchen, bathing room and toilet. Existing Han style Buddhist temples mostly follow the imperial style of China, consisting of several quadrangle dwellings arranged on a symmetrical axis. The main halls are often characterized by side-hall and hip-and-gable roofs. The main buildings on the vertical axis progress from the Gate of the Buddhist Temple, Hall of the Heavenly King, Hall of Great Magnificence and Tower of Buddhist Scriptures, in order.

Most Buddhist buildings in the Tibetan style look square from above. However, in elevation, they are larger at the bottom, tapering toward the top, ending in a flat roof. The exterior of the building features a high wall without visible wood framing, but with windows. Each window is encircled by flat wall decoration; like the whole building, the window frame is not square, but is larger at the bottom and smaller at the top. The lower part of the building is generally painted black. The top is decorated with a circle of parapets, which are colored dark-red with some badge-like decoration made of brass. The common plan is a courtyard in the center, surrounded by wood-structure verandas in two or three layers. The main hall lies in the center at the back of the building, and is the location for the Buddha statue. A big Buddhist temple may appear to consist of several separate stories from the outside, but actually has a tall interior space where an enormous Buddhist statue can be housed.

A unique form of Chinese domestic dwelling, they are derived from the natural cave residences of primitive society. Most of them are seen on the loess plateau, where the land is dry and without many trees. They can be roughly divided into three kinds according to their architectural layout and forms of structure, i.e. cliff-leaning, freestanding and sunken. These variations are due primarily to the local terrain of the specific region. Therefore, cave dwellings can be seen as very adaptable and site specific.

English	Chinese	Chinese Pinyin	Image
City-gate towers	城楼	chenglou	
Courtyard houses	院落式民居	yuanluoshi minju	
Tulou (Earth Building)	土楼民居	tulou minju	
Etiquette-oriented buildings	礼制建筑	lizhi jianzhu	
Grottoes	石窟	shiku	

Description

Referring to towers built on the city-gate, they chiefly served the purpose of defense while also adding magnificence to the city and creating a sense of drama to the entrance. In ancient China, most cities had a tower built on the gate. In the period from the Eastern Han (25 – 220) to the Sui dynasty (581 – 618), the important city-gate towers were mostly multi-story, with two or three floors most common. However, in the period from the Tang (618 – 907) to the Yuan dynasty (1279 – 1368), most had a single floor. In the Ming and Qing dynasties (1368 – 1911), the number of floors depended on the city's importance; most city-gate towers of ordinary cities had two floors whereas the towers in Beijing were mostly three stories.

Typical traditional Chinese residences, they have a history of 2,000 years. Generally speaking, one courtyard would house one family. Most of these residences faced south, following the traditional belief of ancient China that people were supposed to see the world while facing south. The plan was arranged on an axis, with the ancestral hall set at the back of the center. The ancestral hall was the highest and the most exquisitely decorated building in the complex. Rooms were distributed to family members according to their status and age. In general, rooms on the left (east) were for senior family members while rooms on the right (west) were for juniors. Rooms at the back (north) were for the distinguished, while rooms in the front (south) were for the lower ranking.

These remarkable residential complexes were built with defense and communal living in mind. Called Tulou, or earth buildings, they often were multi-storied and most were built of rammed earth. The greatest number of these buildings can be seen on the junction between eastern Yongding County and western Nanjing County in southwest Fujian Province. There are also a few in the counties of Hua'an, Pinghe, Zhangpu, Yunxiao and Zhaoan in southern Fujian. While most are round, there are also those with a square plan.

An important segment of ancient Chinese architecture, etiquette-oriented buildings, relate to the feudal patriarchal code. They chiefly include altars, temples and ancestral halls, and demonstrate feudal hierarchies, such as the relationship between heaven and human beings, between the classes, and between individuals. In layout and tone, they are most similar to that of religious buildings. Existing examples include the Temple of Heaven, Altar of the Earth, Altar of the Moon, Altar of the Sun, and Shennong Altar.

This is a common type of Buddhist building, where caves are dug out of cliff sides, rather than being freestanding structures. These grottoes are chiefly distributed in Xinjiang Uygur Autonomous Region, Gansu, Shanxi and Henan Provinces. Chinese grottoes enjoy a great number and a long history. There are many large grottoes containing exquisite sculptures that have important historical and artistic value. Although they have distinctive regional features, grottoes in different places did influence one another, forming a somewhat unified grotto art. The most famous examples include Mogao Grottoes in Gansu Province; Yungang Grottoes in Datong of Shanxi Province; Longmen Grottoes in Henan Province; and Dazu Grottoes in Sichuan Province.

English	Chinese	Chinese Pinyin	Image
Private gardens	私家园林	sijia yuanlin	
Royal gardens	皇家园林	huangjia yuanlin	
Royal tombs	皇家陵墓	huangjia lingmu	
Taoist buildings	道教建筑	daojiao jianzhu	

Description

Compared with royal gardens, private gardens came into being later, approximately in the Western Han dynasty (206 BC – AD 25). In their early stages, they followed the style of royal gardens, and private gardens in the true sense appeared only in the Northern and Sothern dynasties (420 – 589). They differed from royal gardens it that they pursued a scholarly appeal, particularly emulating paintings, and existed within a smaller landscape space. In the period from the Sui to the Tang dynasty (581 – 907), the style of private gardens gradually reached maturity, with two peaks of construction: the Song dynasty (960 – 1279) and the Ming and Qing dynasties (1368 – 1911). Among the many noted private gardens are Jingu Garden, built by Shi Chong in the Southern and Northern dynasties, as well as Hu Garden and Dule Garden from the Song dynasty. They all sought to emulate nature in an artistic manner.

Built with funds from the royal family, these gardens were to be enjoyed only by emperors and members of the royal family. The earliest royal gardens date to the Pre-Qin period (prior to 221 BC) during which gardens of this kind were chiefly for the hunting and recreation of emperors. Early gardens did not have exceptional architecture despite their huge areas, but instead, were built to feature outstanding natural scenery and to house a large number of domesticated animals. The Qing dynasty witnessed the peak of royal gardens in China. With a magnificent scale and vast area, they contained buildings for recreation and enjoyment as well as palaces and Buddhist temples. In their architectural forms and color schemes, most bore a strong resemblance to royal palaces, presenting a brilliant and magnificent testament to imperial power.

Elaborate burial ritual derived not only from the filial tradition of devotion of the younger generation to its predecessors, but also the desire to portray the power of the hereditary imperial throne and the dynasty. Therefore, emperors spared no efforts in building huge tombs for themselves, using vast resources in terms of both manpower and materials. These tombs are called "Emperor tombs" or "Empress tombs." As indicated by existing ruins, most Chinese royal tombs follow a layout similar to palace architecture, resembling the places, in which emperors lived in their lifetime. Most were built near the dynasty's capital city. For example, Qian Tomb in the Tang dynasty (618 – 907) was built near Chang'an, the Tang capital, while the Thirteen Imperial Tombs in the Ming dynasty (1368 – 1644) were built near Beijing, the capital at that time.

Native to China, Taoism is derived from folk religion and ancient philosophies, with reverence for ancestors and immortals as key concepts. Taoism upholds Laozi as its founder, advocating his teachings and those of his follower, Zhuangzi. Taoist buildings refer to those for the worshipping of Taoist deities, i.e. palaces and Taoist temples. Some that are devoted chiefly to the worshipping of folk spirits are also called temples. The overall layout follows the traditional courtyard model, and consists of the immortal hall, dining hall, dormitory and garden. The architectural decoration and scale demonstrate the Chinese doctrine of Yin and Yang as well as the Five Elements. Existing Taoist buildings were mostly rebuilt in the Ming and Qing dynasties (1368 – 1911).

English	Chinese	Chinese Pinyin	Image
Wind-rain bridges	风雨桥	fengyu qiao	

Architectural Structures and Components

English	Chinese	Chinese Pinyin	Image
Ancestral halls	祠堂	citang	
Drama stages	戏台	xitai	
Gates with window lattices	隔扇门	geshanmen	

Description

Wind-rain bridges, or covered bridges, come in many varieties, among which those of the Dong minority are the most unique and varied. In addition to a corridor, these bridges feature a pavilion on top of the bridge span, presenting a beautiful scene. Many covered bridges are also seen in southern Zhejiang Province and northern Fujian Province. The covering on these bridges is not as complex as that of the Dong minority bridges, and they have a more antique and simpler form of wooden arch.

Description

The ancestral hall is the place where a family clan offers sacrifice and reverence to its predecessors. In addition, it has many other purposes, including marriages, funerals, festivals and birthday celebrations. It is also the venue for members of the family to discuss important affairs. In a village, the scale of the ancestral hall is larger than that of residential houses, and it is marked by high architectural quality and meticulous decoration. The ancestral hall is generally built within a village. It can also be part of a large residential complex with related family clans, such as in the earth buildings, or Tulou, of Fujian Province.

In ancient China, drama stages could be found in both royal palaces and the villages of common folk. Prior to the Tang dynasty (618 – 907), drama performances took place on a simple open-air platform or a building with basic viewing sheds. In the Tang dynasty, a type of specialized music shelter built especially for performance appeared. Chinese drama became mature in the Song dynasty (960 – 1279), as did the architecture of the performance venues. In the Yuan dynasty (1279 – 1368), venues for performance developed into different types, such as dance-halls, music towers and opera stages. The Ming and Qing dynasties (1368 – 1911) saw dramas performed mostly in the tea-house, and as a result, the venue for performance was then generally called "Tea-house." Finally, theaters exclusively for performance gradually emerged.

First appearing in the Song dynasty (960 – 1279), this type of gate was often seen in later dynasties. They are notable for the window lattices in the upper part, where window paper or gauze paper could be pasted. There are various kinds of window lattices. The lower part of the gate is made of solid wood carved with plants, flowers, auspicious birds and animals or other kinds of symbolic and beautiful patterns. The gate and the window are in a proportion of about 4:1 or even greater, creating a slender form. A gate of this kind could have four, six or eight windows, chiefly based on the size of the standard width of the associated building.

English	Chinese	Chinese Pinyin	Image
House-like gates	屋宇式大门	wuyushi damen	
Memorial gateways	牌坊	paifang	
Pavilion	亭	ting	
Caisson ceiling	藻井	zaojing	

Description

A major type of gates, this took the shape of an independent house, i.e. a gate as well as a complete structure in and of itself. Gates of this kind were seen in many types of buildings in ancient China, extensively applied in royal palaces as well as common residences. They are two chief different forms, the first being a completely independent "gate-house" mainly applied to official buildings, and the second, a "passage" linking a row of buildings in front of the courtyard with the exit and entrance, which appeared mainly in domestic dwellings.

This structure was chiefly composed of pillars or columns, stones lying against pillars, and different types of beams. Commonly having two or four pillars, some of the big memorial gateways had up to eight pillars. In addition to having different sizes, they could also be erected in different locations, such as a mausoleum, ancestral hall, garden, or even by the roadside. They can further be classified into three kinds according to their different functions: memorial gateway of a landmark, memorial gateway of virtue, and memorial gateway of rigorous female chastity.

An architectural form most representative of traditional Chinese buildings, the pavilion has a long history, tracing back to as early as the Shang and Zhou dynasties (1600 – 256 BC). Originally a rest place for travelers, it evolved constantly, gradually becoming rich in its functions and forms. Before the Han dynasty (206 BC – AD 25), pavilions still served primarily as a place for travelers to rest or as places for sending warnings, and the size was fairly large. It was not until the Wei and Jin dynasties that small pavilions for tourism came into being. In the Northern and Southern dynasties (420 – 589), people began to build pavilions in parks in an extensive way, hence replacing the pavilion's practical function with a more aesthetic one. After the Tang and Song dynasties (618 – 1279), pavilions became more diversified and great attention was given to form and decoration. Hence later pavilions have small size and rich patterns as two typical features.

This coffered ceiling in an arc form that covers the internal support structure of the roof when viewed from inside the building. Each component of such a ceiling is a recessed wood panel decorated with patterns, relief and/or paintings, hence the name "sunken panel." This type of ceiling was only applied to distinguished buildings—for example, above a Buddha statue or the imperial throne—and was rarely used in buildings for common folk.

Roof Types

English	Chinese	Chinese Pinyin	Image
Cuanjian Ding	攒尖顶	cuanjian ding	
Hip-and-gable roof	歇山顶	xieshan ding	
Juanpeng Ding	卷棚顶	juanpeng ding	
Side-hall roof	庑殿顶	wudian ding	

Description

This type of roof has only vertical ridges, with the number of ridges determined according to the needs of actual structure. Generally speaking, the ridges occurred mostly in even numbers, usually four ridges, six ridges and eight ridges, which were called four-angled Cuangjian Ding, six-angled Cuangjian Ding and eight-angled Cuangjian Ding respectively. There is also a kind of circular Cuangjian Ding.

A hip-and-gable roof has a total of nine ridges. The horizontal ridge meets with two main vertical ridges on either end to form a triangular peak. There are also four slanting ridges that extend out from the bottom corners of the two triangles. The gable portion of the roof rises elegantly up to the top, with the hip below slanting gracefully outward.

This type of roof is also called a Sycee-shaped ridge, after a type of Chinese silver or gold ingot coin. The junction between the front and the back of the roof is turned into an arc curve instead of a ridge, or ordinary " 人 -shaped" roof. An example is in Xiequ Park in the Summer Palace in Beijing, where the roofs of all buildings are in the shape of Juanpeng Ding.

It has a main horizontal ridge with two vertical ridges curving outward from each end. The four sides of the roof top also slant outward with a graceful curvature, making this type of roof special. In fact, the side-hall roof is of the highest grade in terms of roofs in ancient Chinese buildings, and was only applied to the most distinguished buildings, such as palaces and the halls of Buddhist temples. Existing buildings with this type of roof were mostly built in the Ming and Qing dynasties (1368 – 1911), among which the most famous is Taihe Hall in the Forbidden City (now the Palace Museum in Beijing).

Copy by the author showing a city in the Qi State in the Warring States period

CHAPTER 1

PRE-QIN ERA

Prior to its unification for the first time under the Qin dynasty (221 – 210 BC), China had gone through three dynasties, the Xia (c. 2100 – 1600 BC), Shang (c. 1600 – 1047 BC) and Zhou (1046 – 256 BC), controlling varying portions of what we know now as China. The earliest populations in China were located in the northern area centering on the Yellow River Basin.

Despite its remoteness in time, the historical record of the Zhou dynasty is known through ancient Chinese literature that describes the time, place, circumstances and figures for many major historical events. For example, we know that in 770 BC the King of Ping moved the capital from Haojing in the west to Luoyang in the east. This established the Eastern Zhou dynasty (770 – 256 BC), which ruled alongside numerous rival states, no longer receiving regular devotion, tribute or duty visits from many kingdoms. From then until the establishment of the Qin dynasty, there was a long period of almost constant warfare, with major consolidations under the Spring and Autumn period (770 – 476 BC) and the Warring States period (475 – 221 BC).

Over the long period prior to the Qin dynasty, Chinese architecture developed in the north from primitive cave dwellings to more sophisticated cave houses and ground post and lintel construction. In the south, the "nest" building or shack-like structure developed into stilt-style dwellings with elevated ground floors.

Archaeological discoveries have provided much insight into court architecture. Recent discoveries of the ancient ruins of Shang dynasty palaces include the site of the Shang city, Shixianggou, in Yanshi, Henan Province; the site of the Shang city of Zhengzhou, in Henan; and the palace ruins from the Late Shang dynasty in Anyang, Henan. From these ruins, the basic form

Copy by the author of a panorama view of the Zhongshan Princess's cemetery in the Warring States period. The original piece was drawn by Fu Xi'nian.

of a Shang dynasty palace has been determined. This layout features an "outer court and inner palace" in an early form, with the building where the ruler dealt with state affairs located in the front, and his living chamber in the rear. The many following dynasties all adopted this layout in constructing their palaces.

Great achievements were made in urban construction during the Zhou dynasty (1046 – 256 BC). Above all, the planning and construction of the capital had a profound effect on the architecture of succeeding dynasties. The Zhou capital city plan is square, with three city gates on the sides. There are transversal and longitudinal roads, which lead to the city gate. The ruler's palace lies at the center of the city. In front of the palace, the Imperial

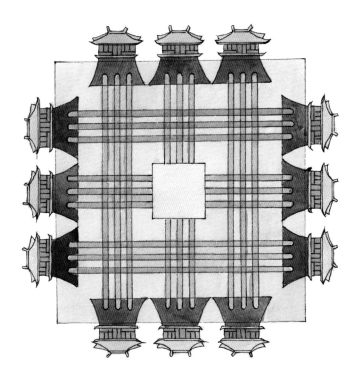

Planning map for the capital of the Zhou dynasty

Ancestral Temple is built on the left side to pay respect to ancestors, and the Altar of Land and Grain is built on the right side to worship the God of Land and God of Grain to promote national stability and prosperity. This basic pattern was used by the following dynasties.

The Eastern Zhou dynasty is divided into two periods: the Spring and Autumn period and Warring States period. During this time, slave society collapsed and feudal society came into being, and there was a cultural florescence. With the turmoil of war, architecture developed slowly in general. However, high-platform building was developing fast. A major representative of this type of architecture is the tomb for the King of Zhongshan during the Warring States period.

CHAPTER 2

THE QIN AND HAN DYNASTIES

In 221 BC, Yingzheng (also known as Qin Shihuang or the First Emperor of Qin, 246 – 209 BC) emerged victorious over the other six factions, bringing the Warring States period to an end and unifying China. The young and aggressive ruler was eager to establish a new title for himself. In the Spring and Autumn and the Warring States periods, the leader of each kingdom referred to himself as "Lord" or "King." Yingzheng believed his feats to be beyond compare, and the title "King" insufficient to match his merits and virtues. Therefore, he conferred on himself the title of emperor. Since he was the first such ruler of a unified China, Yingzheng is referred to as the First Emperor.

In order to consolidate the empire, the First Emperor of Qin adopted a series of reform measures to abolish the ruling system of individual fiefdoms that existed Spring and Autumn and Warring States periods. Instead, he implemented a system that divided the whole country into thirty six commanderies, controlled by imperial officials, under a central power. He unified units of measurements and currency and standardized written language. He also had the Great Wall extended and consolidated to over 2,500 miles, providing a defense against invasion by tribes in the north.

The cultural and architectural achievements of the Qin dynasty are precious, but carried a great cost for the common people at that time. For example, thousands upon thousands of peasants and prisoners were forced to rebuild the Great Wall on the desert northern border for over ten years, many dying of fatigue and sickness. The ruthlessness, extortion and tyranny of the Qin dynasty led to its downfall.

During the first year of the second Qin Emperor, two conscripted laborer, Chen Sheng and Wu Guang, who were to be executed following an unavoidable delay in a project for which they were responsible, led an uprising and made themselves kings. In the same year, Liu Bang also launched an uprising and made himself Lord of Pei. In 206 BC, Liu Bang led his troops into Bashang (currently east of Xi'an, Shaanxi Province), where Ziying, nephew of the second Qin Emperor, who served as king of Qin after his uncle died for less than two months, surrendered and the Qin dynasty perished. Thus began the Han dynasty (206 BC – AD 220), which is divided into two periods: Western Han dynasty (206 BC – AD 25) and Eastern Han dynasty (25 – 220).

From the view of Chinese architectural history, the Han dynasty represents the first true highpoint, building on and improving the fine tradition it inherited, and greatly influencing future development. Compared with the Qin dynasty, there are a rich variety of building types, such as cities, palaces, tombs, ritual architecture and residences, which achieve full development in this period. Palaces and civic planning represent the highest achievements of architectural technology and craftsmanship of the Han dynasty.

The Great Wall (Qin Dynasty)

The Qin Great Wall extends from Lintao (currently Minxian in Gansu Province) in the west to Liaodong in the east, consisting of new construction during the Qin, and improvement and connecting of walls from previous kingdoms. The type of fortification wall used in different sections depended on the terrain. The Qin Great Wall was mostly built with rammed earth. Walls on a plain or at a pass are towering and solid, while walls at the

The Great Wall

The beacon tower at Yumenguan, Gansu Province

dangerously steep places are low and narrow to save manpower and resources. Gate cities were built at the favorable defending places to use minimal troops to prevent intrusion of powerful enemies. Beacon towers were also built on the Great Wall to ensure that military intelligence could be passed quickly. The method of passing intelligence on the beacon tower consisted of using smoke in the day and fire at night.

After the Qin dynasty, many dynasties continued to build the Great Wall to defend against nomadic tribes from the north. There are many gate cities on the Great Wall, with almost a thousand from the Ming dynasty alone, such as Shanhaiguan, Juyongguan, Jiayuguan and Yanmenguan. The repair and expansion of the Great Wall under following dynasties, such as the Western Han, Northern Wei, Sui, Tang and Ming dynasties, resulted in the Great Wall extending from Jiayuguan Pass (Gansu Province) in the west to Shanhaiguan Pass (Hebei Province) and extending more than 11,000 *li* (a Chinese unit of length equaling a half-kilometer).

The Terracotta Warriors

The Qin dynasty achieved enormous accomplishments within a limited fifteen years, incomparable by dynasties before or after it. There are two important palaces in the Qin dynasty, Xianyang Palace and Epang Palace.

An array of terracotta warriors and horses in the tomb of Qin Shi Huang near Xi'an, Shaanxi Province

Based on evidence in literature and excavated ruins, we know that these two palaces were grand and expansive, representing a climax in ancient palace construction. However, due to the scarcity of literary inscriptions or historical relics, we cannot tell the specific form of their architecture, layout and other details. However, the Terracotta Warriors of the First Emperor, unearthed in 1974, provide clear and ample evidence of the technical achievements and magnificence of architecture in the Qin dynasty.

The Terracotta Warriors are located at Lintong in Shaanxi Province. To date, three vaults have been excavated: the No. 1 vault and No. 2 vault, which are an imitation of large-scale combat formations, and No. 3 vault, which replicates a command center. The Terracotta Warriors serve as important evidence not only for ancient combat formation and tactics, but also for the technical and artistic achievement of the time.

There are over 8,000 Terracotta Warriors, dozens of chariots and almost 10,000 weapons. The scale is about life-size, with figures in various postures such as standing, kneeling and crouching. Cavalry, infantry, chariot warriors, archers and officers are all depicted among the Terracotta Warriors. Since they vary in social status and roles in battle, they wear different clothing, ornaments and weapons. Amazingly, every Terracotta Warrior exhibits a different appearance and characteristics, with incredible detail. The faces are delicately portrayed, representing the great achievements of statuary art in the Qin dynasty.

Copy by the author of *Han Palaces*, which shows a divine mountain on the sea. The original piece was drawn by Yuan dynasty artist Li Rongjin, now preserved in Palace Museum, Taipei.

Han Palaces

Because of the destruction caused by wars at the end of the Qin dynasty, the construction of cities and palaces from the beginning of the Han dynasty is inferior to those of the Qin dynasty. This is the case up until Emperor Wu of the Han dynasty (140 – 88 BC) ordered large-scale construction, including a large number of palaces. Well-known palaces in the Han dynasty include Weiyang Palace, Changle Palace and Jianzhang Palace.

Jianzhang Palace was a temporary imperial palace built in the Imperial Forest Park outside the capital. The Imperial Forest Park was in existence already in Qin dynasty, and was expanded and repaired in the Han dynasty. According to historical records, there were once many temporary imperial palaces in the Imperial Forest Park, with Jianzhang Palace as the largest. Most construction in the palaces is of multi-story buildings with rivers, hills and pools. Three islands—Penglai, Yingzhou and Fangzhang—are built in a pool, which is called "Three Isles in One Pool."

The pattern of "Three Isles in One Pool" dates back to the Qin dynasty but it refers to the legend of Fairy Mountain, which originated even earlier, in Spring and Autumn period and Warring States period. To cater to the kings' eagerness for immortality, alchemists from various regions invented a story about a Fairy Mountain in the East Sea, home to the Gods and to an immortality elixir. Rulers believed the story without a shadow of doubt and

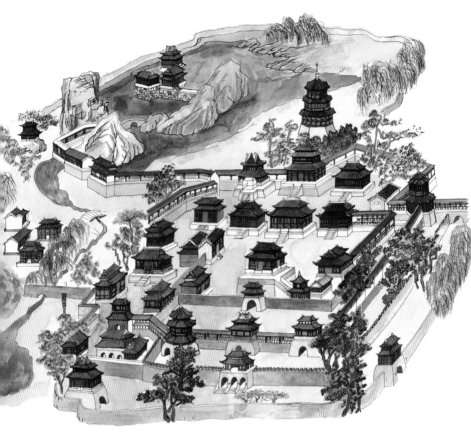

Copy by the author of Jianzhang Palace of the Han dynasty

sent their troops to look for a Fairy Mountain on the sea many times. The First Emperor of Qin also sent his men in search of the immortality elixir on several occasions, but they returned without success. Therefore, he excavated a pool in his own garden (symbolizing the sea) and built three islands in it (which symbolize the Fairy Mountains) to seek psychological comfort.

Jianzhang Palace became a model for imperial gardens in the successive dynasties, which carried on the "Three Isles in One Pool" tradition, and also influenced the landscape layout of other types of gardens.

CHAPTER 3

THE THREE KINGDOMS PERIOD, WESTERN AND EASTERN JIN DYNASTIES, AND NORTHERN AND SOUTHERN DYNASTIES

At the end of the Eastern Han dynasty, officials from various regions raised troops to establish their own armed forces. Cao Cao, the Duke of Wei, basically controlled the northern region, and in 220, his son, Cao Pi, succeeded the throne as King of Wei. In the same year, Emperor Xian, who would be the last emperor of the Eastern Han, stepped down and Cao Pi came to the throne, with Wei as the kingdom name. The next year, Liu Bei came to the throne in Chengdu, with Han as the kingdom name. A few years later, Sun Quan, a general guarding the Jiangdong Districts, came to the throne at Wuchang with Wu as the kingdom name.

When Sun Quan came to the throne, China entered the period of the Three Kingdoms. The more than three centuries from the Three Kingdoms period through the Western and Eastern Jin, and Northern and Southern dynasties are the most disorderly and turbulent in Chinese history. The northern region was especially trapped in chaos caused by wars, and minority groups dominated the vast regions in the Yellow River Basin. The flow of various ethnic groups into this area, along with the ethnic groups at the border, made ethnic relations complicated in this period. While the interactions between ethnic groups led to often devastating wars, they also served to promote economic and cultural exchanges.

Copy by the author of *Wang Xizhi Observing Geese*, which captures a scene from the daily life of Wang Xizhi, a great calligrapher in the Eastern Jin dynasty

White Horse Temple

Buddhism flourished in the Northern and Southern dynasties (420 – 589). The chaos caused by wars made Buddhism appealing to the public, allowing them to look forward to the Western paradise described in Buddhism. On the other hand, the doctrines of Buddhism were also appealing to rulers, allowing them a means of control over the common people. Therefore, they spared no effort or expense to encourage the development of Buddhism. Suddenly, the construction of Buddhist architecture, such as monasteries, temples and grottoes, came to a climax.

The first Buddhist temple, the White Horse Temple of Luoyang (Henan Province), was built as Buddhism was introduced to China in the Eastern Han dynasty (25 – 220). The construction of Buddhist temples continued relatively unchanged until the Northern and Southern dynasties, when it developed more "Chinese" characteristic. Generally speaking, a Chinese Buddhist temple is composed of multiple courtyards and is centered on the main palace hall or pagoda. There is a clear distinction between primary

The gate of White Horse Temple, Luoyang, Henan Province

and secondary buildings and the layout is regular. In this way, the Chinese Buddhist architecture style uses the traditional Chinese architectural layout as the base, adding foreign features like the pagoda, which evolved from the Indian temple stupa.

Cave Temples
(Yungang Grottoes and Longmen Grottoes)

The construction of grottoes, also called cave temples, emerged in the Northern and Southern dynasties. Their main functions are the same as for other Buddhist temples in which the monks practice sermons, erect statues for followers to worship, and hold ceremonies. Chinese grottoes originate in the Eastern Jin dynasty (317 – 420) and last until the Yuan (1206 – 1368) and Ming dynasties (1368 – 1644). Grottoes are most frequent and plentiful during the Northern and Southern dynasties. The Yungang Grottoes of Datong in Shanxi Province and the Longmen Grottoes of Luoyang in Henan Province were all created in the same period.

The Yungang Grottoes, excavated under the rule of Emperor Wencheng

Exterior of the No.9 and No.10 caves of Yungang Grottoes, Datong, Shanxi Province

in the Northern Wei dynasty (453), are located at the Wuzhou Mountain, west of Datong City. The complex consists of 45 grottoes, among which the Five Grottoes of Tanyao (numbered as 16, 17, 18, 19 and 20) are the most famous. Constructed by an eminent monk in the Northern Wei dynasty, the Five Grottoes each contain a giant Buddha as the primary statue. It is said that the five giant Buddhas represent five emperors in the Northern Wei dynasty. The primary Buddha statue is ten meters high; the giant Buddha of No. 20 Grotto is in the open air but remains well preserved.

The plan of the Five Grottoes is U-shaped with a dome top, imitating the style of the thatched cottage in India. The statues share some characteristics with those in India's Ganges River Basin. In later stages, the grotto decoration

Bodhisattva statues, dating to the Northern Zhou dynasty, on the front and left walls of the No. 62 Grotto of the Maijishan Grottoes in Gansu Province

The No. 9 Grotto of Yungang Grottoes, Datong, Shanxi Province

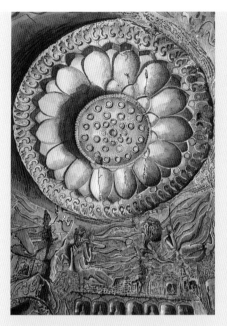

The caisson ceiling in Lianhua Cave at the Longmen Grottoes, Henan Province

Detail of the cross-legged Bodhisattva, located in the eastern shrine on the second floor, northern front chamber, of the No.9 Grotto at the Yungang Grottoes, Datong, Shanxi Province

was influenced by a native painting style promoted by southern artists including Gu Kaizhi and Lu Tanwei. Statues in some grottoes have handsome features and clear contour of eyes and brow. The costumes also have native characteristics, related directly to the "Loose Garment and Long Band" style of the literati and officialdom in the Southern dynasties (420 – 589).

Besides the Five Grottoes of Tanyao, there are some other distinctive grottoes, such as No. 12 Grotto, which features delicate sculpture, the No. 5 and No. 6 Grottoes, and the No. 9 and No. 10, which have been combined. There stone columns in front of the No. 9 and No. 10 Grottoes have been worn away by the wind, although the statues in the colonnades are well preserved. The double-grotto, common in the Northern and Southern dynasties, bears an important feature of grotto construction at that time. This double-grotto with colonnades had two functions. The first is practical, in that it can protect the statues inside. The second is aesthetic, as it resembles the exteriors of wooden architectural structures of that time.

CHAPTER 4

THE SUI AND TANG DYNASTIES

A long-lasting split followed by a reunion, and then the reverse—such stories have been played out repeatedly in Chinese history. After several hundred years of division and turmoil, China again entered into a reunion stage during the Sui and Tang dynasties. Similar to the Qin and Han dynasties, the Sui dynasty (581 – 618) and Tang dynasty (618 – 907) are traditionally studied and discussed together in Chinese history. It is mainly due to the remarkable continuity of the two dynasties. Of course, one dynasty necessarily follows another in time, but it is not often that there is continuity in other aspects, as dynastic change is often accompanied by great upheaval. Economy and culture may have underlying continuity, but architecture often undergoes changes. Generally speaking, the change of dynasties is a process of besieging cities and destroying homes. Therefore, many historical cities and buildings have been destroyed by the succeeding rulers. However, there are unique aspects to the changes from Qin to Han, Sui to Tang, and Ming to Qing, in which we see certain continuity.

The Sui and Tang period is a highly developed period in every aspect, and architecture is also no exception. The solemn, elegant and large-scale buildings represented the magnificence, aspirations and power of the rulers. The huge corbel arch and raised eaves represent technical achievements, depending on the internal tensile force for support. The architecture of the Sui and Tang period symbolizes the maturity of ancient Chinese architecture.

The City of Chang'an

Many cities and palaces were constructed in the 37-year-long reign of

Copy by the author of *Snow Stream*. The original piece was drawn by Wang Wei, a poet and painter in the Tang dynasty.

the Sui dynasty. After the Tang dynasty was founded, the palaces and cities of the Sui dynasty were not destroyed, and many of the original buildings were expanded. Chang'an of the Sui and Tang dynasties is a most typical example.

Yang Jian, Emperor Wen (581 – 601) of the Sui dynasty, had ordered the building of the capital city, Daxing (present-day Xi'an, Shaanxi Province), before he defeated the Chen dynasty (557 – 589) and reunited China. Since Emperor Wen, Yang Jian, had previously been given the title, "Lord of Daxing" (meaning "great and prosperous"), he called his capital Daxing City, the palace town, Daxing Palace, and the main hall, Daxing Hall.

In the Tang dynasty, the city was renamed Chang'an (meaning "safe and sound forever") and expanded, keeping its basis in the original architecture. The two most prominent changes include 1) Daming Palace built in the north of the city by Emperor Gaozong of the Tang dynasty (650 – 683); and 2) Xingqingfang, the palace where Emperor Xuanzong (712 – 742) lived as a prince and which he rebuilt. Otherwise, there was almost no change.

Chang'an was gigantic in scale,
and one of the most prosperous cities in the
world at that time. It had a highly orderly layout,
with clear functions and divisions. Chang'an of the Tang
dynasty was divided into three sections: the outer town, imperial
town and palace town. The palace town, located at the city center, is
where the emperor administered state affairs. The imperial town, outside the
palace town, is where relatives of the emperor and government officers lived.
Civilians lived outside the imperial town. The residential district had a highly
organized pattern, divided into several square or rectangle areas, enclosed
with subdivision walls, called Li or Fang. Li and Fang are fundamental
component units; the size of a city is determined by the number of Fang. A
closed market was built between subdivisions creating a business district, and
roads laid on the square grid between markets and subdivisions (Fang).

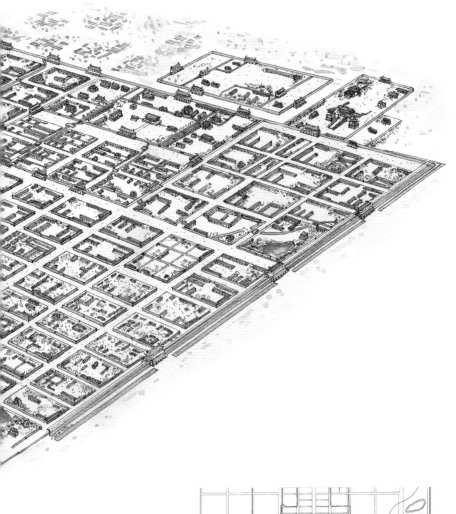

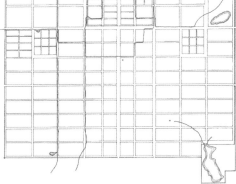

Above: A panorama drawing of Chang'an
in the Tang dynasty

Right: A plan of Daxing City of the Sui
dynasty and the city name was
changed to Chang'an during the
Tang dynasty

Daming Palace

The palaces of the Tang dynasty were, for the most part, inherited from the Sui dynasty, with only the names changed. When Emperor Gaozong (650 – 683) came to the throne, the construction of new palaces was started, namely Daming Palace located in the northeast corner of Chang'an. Daming Palace is in a favorable location, with an invigorating terrain and extensive view. Looking to the south from the Daming Palace, the entire city can be seen. After the Daming Palace was completed, it became the palace most frequently used by emperors of the Tang dynasty. Similar to palaces in previous dynasties, it contained official areas where the emperor would administer state affairs, living chambers, and gardens for the recreation of queens and concubines. The Daming Palace is completely functional in imperial terms.

The Qian Tomb

Ancient emperors took death as seriously as birth; after being revered and living a luxurious life, they would, of course, wish it to continue after their death. Consequently most Chinese emperors placed great importance on building their own tombs before their death. The scale and structure of their tombs are similar to the palaces where they lived, as can be demonstrated by the Qian Tomb of the Tang dynasty. Imperial tombs in the Tang dynasty have both above-ground and underground components. The underground palace was mainly used for housing coffins, while buildings for sacrifice and worship were mostly built above ground.

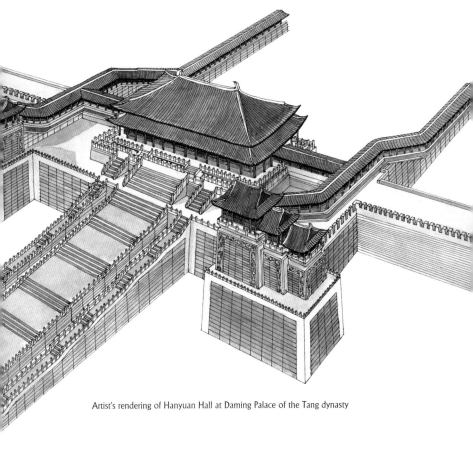

Artist's rendering of Hanyuan Hall at Daming Palace of the Tang dynasty

Section view of the coffin chamber in the tomb of Yongtai Princess

49

Fresco in the tomb of the Yongtai Princess which located at the southeast of the Qian Tomb of the Tang dynasty

The Qian Tomb is the joint burial site of Emperor Gaozong and Empress Wu Zetian, located in what is now Qian County in Shaanxi Province. The layout of Qian Tomb imitates the pattern of the city of Chang'an. It consists of inner city, outer city, Xiangdian—the main above-ground structure where sacrificial ceremonies were held, and annexes.

The wordless monument of Wu Zetian in the Qian Tomb of the Tang dynasty

The above-ground portion of the Qian Tomb starts with a long divine road, with two peaks located at either side, symbolically guarding the tomb. Along the divine road are stone figures and a pair of ornamental pillars. The subjects of stone figures include humans, horses, birds and lions. They stand on each side of the divine road representing power and prestige, while guarding the departed and showing the magnificence of the tomb.

The layout and arrangement of the Qian Tomb had a great influence, becoming a template for imperial tombs. In addition, Shusheng (meaning "extol the merits") monument is found at the Qian Tomb, where it was used to praise the emperor. There is also a wordless monument beside the Shusheng monument, which was erected by the order of Wu Zetian. Wu Zetian did not want to write down her own merits and virtues, leaving the monument blank.

Wu Zetian is the only empress in Chinese history. A strong and often ruthless ruler, she has received both praise and criticism, making it is difficult to make a final assessment of her place in history. However, the Tang dynasty

Panorama of the Tang dynasty Qian Tomb in Qian County, Shaanxi Province

continued to thrive during the reign of Wu Zetian, which marked a transition between two successful periods, the "Golden Years of Zhenguan" and "Flourishing Period of Kaiyuan."

The Great Hall of Foguang Temple and Nanchan Temple

Economic strength, political stability and a flowering culture mark the Tang dynasty as one of the most powerful epochs in world history. Due to its open policy, there were frequent exchanges with many countries. In this way, the culture of the Tang dynasty became widespread, influencing many neighboring countries. Above all, the architecture of the Tang dynasty had a profound influence on that of Japan, where there are some Tang-style buildings that have been preserved until today.

In China, there are also still a few preserved wooden architectural structures, among which the Great Hall of Foguang Temple and the Main Hall of Nanchan Temple, on Wutai Mountain in Shanxi, are most influential. The two temples are located near Chang'an, the capital of the Tang dynasty, where most temples were built, according to literature.

The Great Hall of Foguang Temple (built in 857) is a great achievement of architecture, exhibiting harmony in plan, structure, appearance and interior, and is a masterpiece of functionality and beauty. It adopts the highest form of roof in ancient Chinese architecture, the hip roof. Both ends of the main ridge of the roof are decorated with *chiwen*, a legendary figure with the power to make rain. The decoration was designed to protect the temple from fire. This type of protective decoration has existed in ancient Chinese architecture since the Han dynasty, lasting to the Ming and Qing dynasties, with only names and images changed in each dynasty.

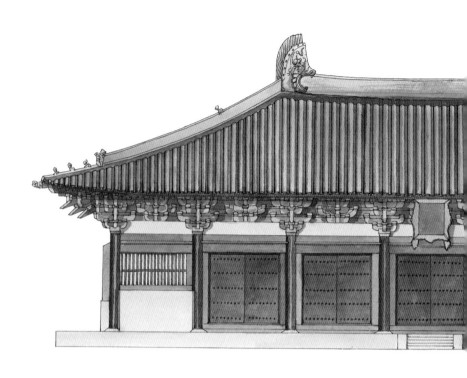

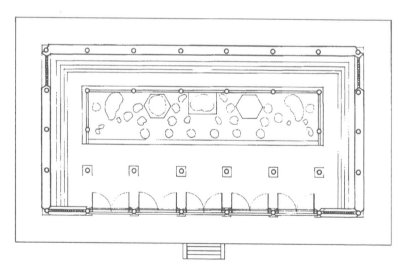

Top: The front elevation of eastern Great Hall, Foguang Temple, Wutai Mountain, Shanxi Province
Bottom: Plan of eastern Great Hall, Foguang Temple

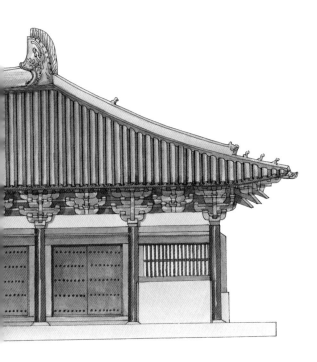

The *chiwen* of the Great Hall of Foguang Temple is elegant, echoing harmoniously with the curve of the roof. Under the eaves is a huge corbel arch, which is used to support the roof. Double-leaf doors are used for entry to the building and the windows adopt mullions, embodying the characteristic dignity of temple halls of the Tang dynasty.

The Great Hall of Nanchan Temple (built in 782), also an architectural treasure of the Tang dynasty, exhibits a lower profile and belongs to the hall system of architecture, while the Great Hall of Foguang Temple belongs to the palace system.

Dayan Pagoda of Ci'en Temple

During the Tang dynasty, the Buddhist pagoda burgeoned prodigiously. While wooden pagodas made up the majority of pagodas in

Dayan Pagoda in Xi'an, Shaanxi Province

Sectional and perspective view of Ci'en Temple in Chang'an (present-day Xi'an)

the Tang dynasty, the pagodas still in existence are usually made of bricks, due to wood's lack of durability over time. The main features of pagodas in the Tang dynasty are: 1) a square plan; and 2) the dominance of pavilion and compact eaves.

The existing Dayan Pagoda of Ci'en Temple in Xi'an in Shanxi Province sheds light on Tang pagoda architecture. It is said that the Dayan Pagoda was constructed by an eminent monk, Xuanzang, to store the Buddhist scriptures he brought from India. The pagoda is ten stories high, with each floor divided into many rooms. The plan is square, but in the elevation view, it is narrow at the top and wide at the bottom, forming a taper. While the pagoda's stable body is built of brick, its form imitates the structure of traditional wood buildings.

CHAPTER 5

THE SONG, LIAO AND JIN DYNASTIES

Historically, the years between the collapse of the Tang dynasty in 907 and the founding of the Song dynasty in 960 are collectively called the Five Dynasties and Ten States. While the north was dominated by insurgencies by semi-nomadic tribes from the steppes, the south was ruled by a series of short military dictatorships. In the north, Yelü Abaoji was able to unify several tribes of the Qidan in 907, and came to the throne in 916. Afterwards, he changed the dynastic name to Liao (907 – 1125). With the support of the Northern Song (960 – 1126), in 1125, another semi-nomadic people overthrew the Liao dynasty, establishing the Jin dynasty (1125 – 1234). Shortly after joining forces with the Song, however, the Jin forced the Song court to flee southward, and the capital of the Southern Song (1127 – 1279) was established in what is now Hangzhou.

Not surprisingly, during this period of frequent changes of power, the social economy and culture were affected. Meanwhile, the rise of northern minority groups resulted in the diversification of the styles and types of buildings in this period. The most prominent architecture of the period is religious buildings.

Buddhism was dominant in the Song, Liao and Jin dynasties, overshadowing Taoism and other religions. While the Song promoted Buddhism to some extent, the Liao and Jin emperors showed much stronger support of Buddhism. Coming from northern nomadic groups, rather than the Han majority, these rulers were eager to use Buddhism, which had long been part of Han culture, to govern Han groups. Therefore, religious buildings in the Liao and Jin period are much more prevalent than those of the Song dynasty, especially those built by royalty. From the evidence of existing examples, we see that most religious buildings were built and rebuilt

Copy by the author of *The Garden in Spring*, demonstrating the architecture of the imperial garden in the Song dynasty

Houtu Temple, in Fenyin, Wanrong County, Shanxi Province, was built according to the highest standards, representing ritual system architecture of the Song dynasty.

under the Liao and Jin rulers.

Unification under the Song dynasty was realized by eliminating the Five Dynasties and Ten States (907 – 960). The kings of the five dynasties and ten states were either taken prisoners by the Song emperor or killed. This called into question the previously unshakable belief in the divine rule of kings, and shook up Chinese feudal society. Under the Song, there was growth in urban life during which the social makeup of China fundamentally changed. There was a florescence in trade and in the arts, and the ritual architecture of the Song dynasty also developed profoundly.

There are mainly two types of ritual architecture in the Song dynasty, the ancestral temple and the altar. The altar was usually built in the open air in the form of a high earth platform without halls or palaces. The ancestral temple, on the other hand, was usually built as architectural group based on axes with a pattern of main and secondary palaces.

Dule Temple

The most typical architecture of the Liao dynasty is the Guanyin (Goddess of Mercy) Cabinet of Dule Temple, along with its mountain gate, in Ji County, and the main hall and the Bhagavad Sutra Hall of the Huayan Temple in Datong.

Dule Temple now has only the mountain gate and the Guanyin Cabinet existing from the Liao dynasty, while the rest of the complex dates to the Ming (1368 – 1644) and Qing (1644 – 1911) dynasties. Although the mountain gate was built during the Liao dynasty, it represents the style of the great Tang dynasty to a large extent. It has a low platform base with a simple body, wood door and window. The burly eave columns completely expose the corbel bracket. While time has worn away the ornate color, these ancient brackets are still strong enough to provide support. Upon entering the gate, one can see the Guanyin Cabinet, neither overly sheltered nor exposed; it has obviously been measured and designed meticulously.

The Guanyin Cabinet has three stories, but only two are observed from outside. The appearance of the Guanyin Cabinet is very special, having features of both the Tang and Song dynasties. The columns in each story are slightly drawn inward to accommodate the low stylobate. Around the lower eave are flat seats while the upper layer roof is

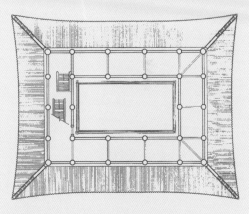

Plan of Guanyin Cabinet of Dule Temple, Ji County, Tianjin

Guanyin (Goddess of Mercy) Cabinet of Dule Temple, Ji County, Tianjin

Eleven Guanyin statues are ensconced in the Guanyin Cabinet of Dule Temple.

of a gable and hip type with a mild slope.

The cabinet's walls are decorated with beautiful paintings. A gigantic Guanyin statue, built in the Liao dynasty, occupies the entire cabinet, with the head of the statue reaching to only just over one meter from the caisson on the top. When one enters the gate, one needs to look up to see the head of Guanyin. This main Guanyin statue is the heaviest one still existing from ancient China. The Guanyin statue possesses a strong Tang dynasty style, plump in shape and rich in color. The structure of the Guanyin Cabinet is proportional, with each part in harmony. It has withstood earthquakes over the centuries, exhibiting the technical achievement of the ancient architects.

The Mahavira Palace at Huayan Temple. It is built on a huge stylobate with a spacious platform in the front, characteristic of Liao and Jin architecture.

Huayan Temple

Huayan Temple in Datong of Shanxi Province was built during the Liao and Jin dynasties. It is situated on the west and faces the east, which is different from the typical arrangement for Han temples, which were situated in the north, facing south. This may be the result of different national religions. The northern minorities worshiped the sun, and so the east, where the sun rises, is the most prestigious. The Han nationality respected the south as the noble seat, therefore, most Han palaces, government buildings and temples are facing south, with the gate opening to the south.

The main existing buildings of Huayan Temple are the Mahavira Hall, built in the Jin dynasty, and the Bhagavad Sutra Hall, built in the Liao dynasty. The Mahavira Hall is built on a huge stylobate with a spacious platform protruding in the front. It is one of the prominent features of Liao and Jin architecture to have a protruding platform in the front of the hall. The roof of the hall has a mild slope, and is simple and stalwart in style. Fewer

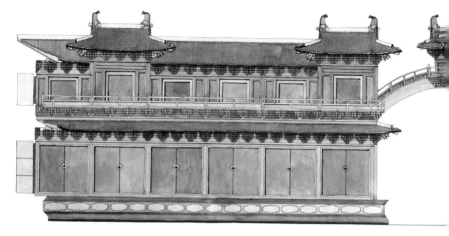

The Bhagavad Sutra Hall at Huayan Temple, Datong, Shanxi Province

columns are used in the hall, providing spacious room for offerings to the Buddha statue and paying tribute to it. Such openness is one of the main features of Liao and Jin architecture.

Typically, large temples of the Liao and Jin dynasties always had scripture halls built especially for storing classics. The Bhagavad Sutra Hall in the Huayan Temple is such a scripture hall, contains the earliest ancient Chinese collection of classics in existence. The hall is typical of the Liao dynasty style, with an extending eave, raised on a slight angle, giving a clear and concise appearance. Over 30 delicate statues of the Liao dynasty are stored in the hall. Among them is one renowned as the "Eastern Venus," i.e. the Bodhisattva, with hands palm-to-palm and grinning, looking lively and delicate.

The Bodhisattva known as the "Oriental Venus" in the Bhagavad Sutra Hall at Huayan Temple

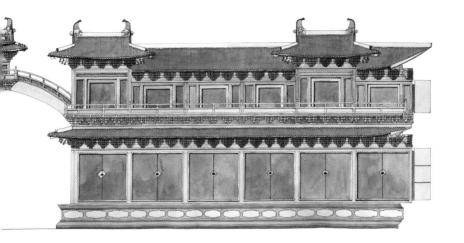

The Longxing Temple

The Longxing Temple of Zhengding in Hebei Province is one of the most important temples of the Song dynasty that is still in existence. While it was built in the Sui dynasty, and rebuilt in later dynasties, it was most frequently maintained in the Song dynasty. Therefore, it exhibits the architectural features of the Song dynasty. The Longxing Temple has an integrated plan with clear axes, precise symmetry and clear strata, showing the maturity of Song temple design.

The Moni Hall in the temple is one of the earliest wooden buildings of the Song dynasty still existing. The building is huge, adopting heavy eaves and a hip-and-gable roof. The rooftop utilizes grey pan tile with green azure stone trimming, while the hall ridge and the ornamentation are made of green azure stone. The most distinctive feature of the Moni Hall is its plan, in the shape of a cross. This variation from a regular square plan is quite beautiful.

While the Moni Hall exhibits singular architecture in terms of its shape, the Dabeige Cabinet at the back of the temple and the two buildings on either side form the most special architectural combination in the temple.

Altar Hall and Cishi Pavilion at Longxing Temple, Zhengding, Hebei Province

The plan of these three buildings shows symmetry, with the main hall in the center and the other two halls as wings. Linking them is an elevated arch bridge, like a flying rainbow, looking even more nimble and pretty among the steady and solid pavilions. Such an exquisite combination derives from the Song dynasty carpenters' mastery of design and construction, representing the superior technical level of Song architecture.

The Wood Pagoda in Ying County

Another important type of Buddhist building is the pagoda. The two Song dynasties (Northern and Southern) represent the apex for the development of the brick and stone pagoda, particularly the pavilion-style pagodas, which developed most rapidly and were widely distributed in this period. Four notable pavilion-style brick-body and wood-structured pagodas are: the Pagoda at Bao'en Temple in Suzhou, Jiangsu Province; the Pagoda at Yunju Temple in Huqiushan; the Liuhe Pagoda in Hangzhou, Zhejiang Province; and the Leifeng Pagoda in Hangzhou, which has collapsed.

Most notable during this period is the wood pagoda in Ying County, Shanxi Province. This wood pagoda enjoys several singular features among

Wood Pagoda, Ying County, Shanxi Province

Wood Pagoda, Ying County, Shanxi Province

China's ancient pagodas. It is the only wood-structure pagoda currently existing in China, its diameter is the largest among existent ancient pagodas, and it is the tallest wood pagoda in the ancient world. For over nine hundred years, the wood pagoda has braved wind and rain, earthquakes and wars, but remains intact. The wood pagoda in Ying County represents the most marvelous technical achievement of China's ancient high-story wood architecture.

Jin Ancestral Temple

The Jin Ancestral Temple is typical of the Song dynasty's ancestral temples. While it was built before the Northern Wei dynasty (386 – 534) by a later generation to memorialize the son of Zhou Wuwang, Tang Shuyu, it was expanded in the Song dynasty. Shengmu (Tang Shuyu's mother) Hall and Yuzhao Feiliang are works of this period.

Jin Ancestral Hall is located at the foot of Xuanweng Mountain in southwestern Taiyuan, Shanxi Province. The surroundings are beautiful, with clear water and a wonderful mountain. Inside the hall, the architecture is nimble and free, in harmony with its environment.

The structure of Shengmu Hall demonstrates a high technical level. Inside, the number of columns was reduced to enlarge the internal space and provide room for enshrining sculptures. Shengmu Hall is outstanding not only in terms of architecture but also the high level of artistry of its sculpture. A gigantic shrine was set in the hall for worship of the main statue

Shengmu Hall and Xian Hall, with the Yuzhao Feiliang (fish pool and flying bridge), at the Jin Ancestral Temple in Taiyuan, Shanxi Province

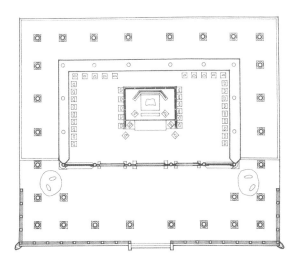

Plan of Shengmu Hall at the Jin Ancestral Temple

The buildings in Jin Ancestral Temple, Taiyuan, Shanxi Province

of the Sacred Mother, around which are 42 colored sculptures of female attendants. These are among the best works of the Song for their proportions, magnificent clothes and lively postures.

The Yuzhao Feiliang in front of Shengmu Hall is a wonder among ancient bridges. Yuzhao means fish pool, in particular, a square-shaped pond; Feiliang (flying beam) is a bridge over the pool. Built in the shape of a cross, the main body of the bridge is flat, with two wings stretching out from below the central portion, looking like a flying swallow. It sits on 34 small octagonal stone pillars set in the water on stone-carved lotus blossoms. The surface is covered with bricks with stone railings lining the sides. The exquisite sculptural quality of Yuzhao Feiliang and its combination of building materials are very rare in the history of ancient Chinese bridges, and it represents an outstanding example of Song dynasty architecture.

Song Royal Gardens

Compared with those of the Sui and Tang dynasties, the gardens of the Song dynasty are more delicate and show a clear development from being

Copy by the author of *Jinming Pool Dragon Boat Race*. It depicts this race held every year in Jinming Pool, a famous imperial garden in the Song dynasty.

merely practical to, instead, focusing on enjoyment. The Song dynasty was known for its emphasis on literature and for deemphasizing the martial arts. The position of intellectuals was higher than in any other dynasty in Chinese history. Therefore, the flourishing of culture in the Song dynasty was unprecedented. At this time, the rise and development of mountain and water paintings, as well as poetry on these subjects, influenced the development of gardens. Many intellectuals personally participated in building gardens, adding poetic and artistic touches.

The most famous royal gardener of the Song dynasty was Emperor Song Huizong (1101 – 1119), who was personally involved the design of the garden, Gengyue (meaning "a garden in the northeast of the capital city"). Song Huizong was an intellectual, skilled at both writing and drawing, and he added elegance to the landscape of Gengyue.

As a representative of Song dynasty gardens, Gengyue set an example for future royal gardens by removing the mountain and filling up the sea, formerly required items. Since then, the royal garden was no longer limited to the scope of purely imitating the mountain and water. Instead it paid more attention to the creation of an artistic landscape, and the pursuit of imagination became fundamental to the gardening arts in China.

CHAPTER 6

THE YUAN DYNASTY

The Yuan dynasty (1279 – 1368) is the first unified dynasty in Chinese history ruled by a minority. The Mongolian nationality, famous for war and exploration over large territory, founded the dynasty that ruled the largest territory in the Chinese feudal period. The foreign rulers, upon entering central China, absorbed aspects of Han culture while also maintaining certain Mongolian national cultural features.

After Yuanshizu Kublai Khan (1215 – 1294) moved the capital city from Shangdu (within present-day Inner Mongolia) to Dadu (present-day Beijing), the Mongolians at first basically retained their native custom of residing in tents. However, with the political rule growing gradually more stable and in need of royal rituals, a formal capital city and palace was required to show power and strength. The Yuan dynasty capital city of Dadu and its palace were built under just such circumstances.

The Mongolians originally believed in Shaman teachings, later gradually accepting Buddhism during their fight against Jin (1115 – 1234). After the Yuan dynasty unified the country, Kublai Khan honored the head of Tibetan Buddhism, Shasijiawa lama, as the "Emperor's Master," and Basiba lama as the "National Master," declaring Buddhism as the official religion. With the endorsement of the Yuan dynasty rulers, Tibetan Buddhism developed rapidly.

A golden saddle with deer patterns of Yuan dynasty

Tibetan Buddhism is also called "Lama Teachings," with "Lama" meaning "Master." The Yuan rulers honored the Lama teachings as the national religion and built related architecture on a large scale. Therefore, not only are there such typical Lama buildings such as Shajia Temple and Xialu Temple in Tibet, but also many Lama buildings in central Han regions, for example, Wan'an Temple in Dadu, the present-day Miaoying Temple pagoda in Beijing.

At the same time that Tibetan Buddhism was endorsed by Yuan rulers, they also supported Taoism. Taoism, China's native religion, founded by Laozi, derives from folk beliefs and ancient philosophies. When the monk, Qiu Chuji (1148 – 1227), visited the first emperor in the Yuan dynasty in order to publicize Laozi's teachings, he was warmly welcomed, and Taoism was granted the privilege of freedom from duties. Taoism reached its peak in the Yuan dynasty, and many Taoist buildings were erected. Taoist architecture adopted the plan of traditional Chinese architecture with clear axes and layers, quite similar to that of temple buildings.

Dadu Capital City

While the Yuan dynasty capital Dadu was a new city, its plan and design were influenced by some capital cities and palaces of former dynasties. The new Dadu city had an almost square plan, consisting of a palace city, imperial city and outer city. The outer city was surrounded by the Hucheng River, serving as a moat, with huge turrets built on each corner of the city walls. Three doors opened to the east, west and south while two doors opened to the north. The road leading to the city gate served as the main road, and lanes connected the main road with all kinds of temples, government buildings, shops and residential communities scattered as if figures on a chessboard. The city boasted underground sewage, constructed below surface before the

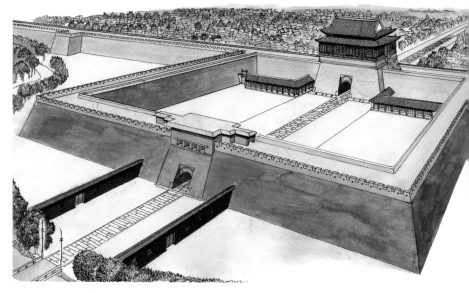

Genghis Khan unified all the Mongolian tribes and gradually established a powerful Mongolian regime, capturing Beijing in 1215.

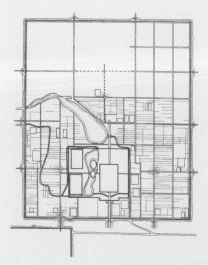

Plan of Dadu (now Beijing), the new capital of the Yuan dynasty

houses and streets were built.

The plan differed from Chang'an's Li and Fang, or enclosed blocks, in that the fifty Fang set up in Dadu were only administrative units. However, such rigorous patterns, streets and buildings certainly possess the taste of the capital city of Tang dynasty.

The new Dadu city exhibited a large scale and overall planning. Its patterning and construction carry on tradition, while also exhibiting a lot of innovation. Among other innovations, what is most special is that Yuan's Dadu takes a lake, Taiyechi, as the center.

Taiye Pond in Dadu is the present-day Beihai Lake, Beijing.

The White Pagoda of Miaoying Temple

During Yuan and Ming dynasties, Lamaist pagodas were built extensively in central China. In this period, the body of the pagoda shrank and featured a more clear demarcation, appearing longer and more delicate. Miaoying Temple's White Pagoda is the biggest and earliest Lamaist pagoda still existing in central China. Designed by the famous Nepali architect, Anigo, the pagoda consists of four parts: base, body, neck and head.

The pagoda base is a one-story platform and a two-story Xumi seat, which means that it comes in at the waist, as if belted. This change from a simple square shape adds beauty characterized by changes of light and shadow. The pagoda body is simple without any extra decoration. Above the pagoda body is a cone-shaped neck,

Miaoying Temple, Beijing

Detail of the Buddhist pedestal, The White Pagoda of Miaoying Temple, Beijing. During the Yuan and Ming dynasties, the body of the pagoda became smaller and more clearly demarcated, looking longer and more exquisite.

with thirteen ridges, representing the thirteen levels of Heaven. The head of the pagoda looks like a straw hat, made in copper. Many bells hang at the edge, blowing in the breeze.

Yonglegong

Yonglegong, which can be found in Shanxi Province, is a precious example of a Yuan dynasty hall building. A typical Yuan Taoist building, it was one of the important posts of the Quanzhen Sect in the Yuan dynasty.

The Sanqing Hall, Yonglegong, Ruicheng, Shanxi Province, is the most important hall in Yonglegong. With its more formal wood structure, it shows high technical achievement and artistic value.

The scale of Yonglegong was originally very large, although now only some main buildings on the central axes remain.

The Sanqing Hall in the main hall is the largest and the space within which it is located is also huge. The hall and houses at the back gradually shrink in scale. This plan complies with the general Taoist style. The Sanqing Hall maintains the basic structural features of the Song dynasty, with the outer columns relatively high and a gentle slope to the rooftop. However, the bucket arch has been simplified, and compared with other wood buildings of the Yuan dynasty, the Sanqing Hall adopts a more formal structure with a higher technical level and artistic value. The wall paintings of the three big halls in the middle of Yonglegong mark a highpoint of Yuan dynasty wall paintings. They are not only grand in scale, but also feature figures that are vivid and fluid.

Fresco in Sanqing Hall, Yonglegong

CHAPTER 7

THE MING DYNASTY

After the Mongolian rule over the Chinese for 162 years, Zhu Yuanzhang led his people in the overthrow of the Yuan dynasty and established the Ming dynasty, with the Han majority in power once again. The capital city was located in Nanjing, the so-called south capital. Zhu Yuanzhang (also known as Hongwu) appointed his 25 sons as vassal kings in different locations throughout China to rule each region, direct the army, and protect the borders, especially to the north.

Before his death, Yuanzhang appointed his grandson, Zhu Yunwen, to be the next emperor. But after he ascended to the throne, Zhu Yunwen (Jianwen) could not control his 25 uncles and decided to cancel the system of vassal states. Zhu's fourth son, Zhu Di, lived in Beijing and commanded a powerful army, which protected the northern border against the Mongolian hordes. He refused to give up his power, becoming instead a rebel force against the central government army.

After a war lasting four years, Zhu Di's army occupied Nanjing. Zhu Di (Yongle Emperor) claimed the illegitimate position as third emperor of the Ming

Scenes of the Capital City shows the bustling city life in Beijing during the Ming dynasty.

Copy by the author of the plan of Nanjing, capital of the Ming dynasty during 1368 — 1421

dynasty. But he was afraid to live in Nanjing and in 1416 he decided to re-establish the capital in Beijing.

The most glorious architectural achievements of the Ming dynasty are the Forbidden City, the Imperial Tombs, several important temples in Beijing, and the further construction of the Great Wall.

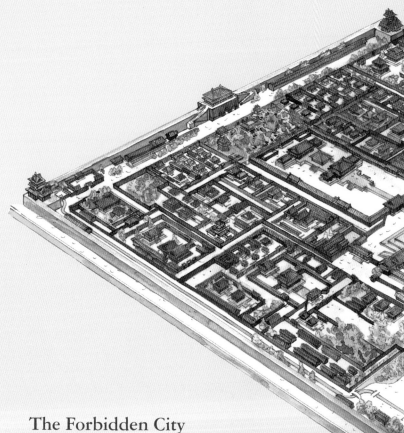

The Forbidden City

The enormous project of constructing the new palace
began in 1406, and Zhu Di lived to see it completed in 1420. The
central government moved formally to Beijing, which had also been the
ruling city of the Mongolian leaders during the Yuan dynasty.

The new Forbidden City remained on the same north-south axis line
as the former palace, but was placed south of the former city center. This
new location in Beijing's center required the relocation of the southern city
wall. While the old city wall was earthen in the Yuan dynasty, during the
new construction the entire city wall was covered in brick. The eastern and
western city walls were 5,350 meters in length and the adjacent walls north
to south measured 6,672 meters. There were nine city gates and each gate

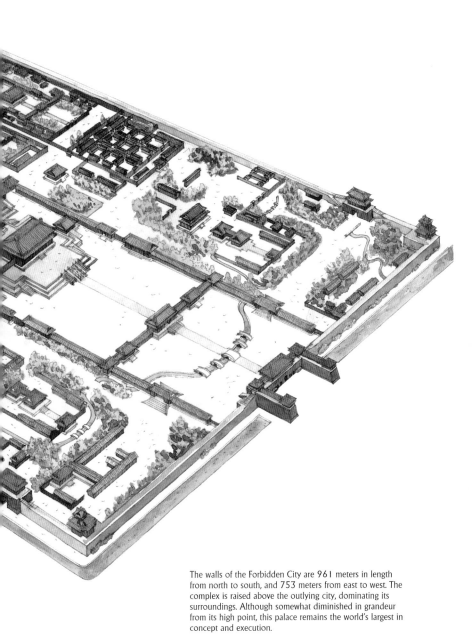

The walls of the Forbidden City are 961 meters in length from north to south, and 753 meters from east to west. The complex is raised above the outlying city, dominating its surroundings. Although somewhat diminished in grandeur from its high point, this palace remains the world's largest in concept and execution.

The three outer buildings occupied the absolute center and were built on a three-tiered pavilion fronted by an enormous square. No trees or other tall elements were allowed in this courtyard so as to provide the safest, most austere environment.

had a barbican entrance, with guard towers to protect the city. A moat, 30 meters wide and five meters deep surrounded the city wall at a distance of 50 meters from the outer side. L-shaped buildings stood three stories high at each corner of the wall with windows suitable for archers. In addition to their defensive role, these fortress corners also served to decorate and unify the wall as an integral structure.

Residences, public houses and religious temples surrounded the central jewel, the Forbidden City. Between the outer city and the Forbidden City stood the emperor's city, 2,750 meters by 2,500 meters, walled with several gates. The southern gate located at the axis line of the wall of the emperor's city was named Tian'an Men gate. Lying to the north of Tian'an Men Square, it is the most famous Chinese gate in modern times. The emperor's city was comprised of government department houses, emperor's storage,

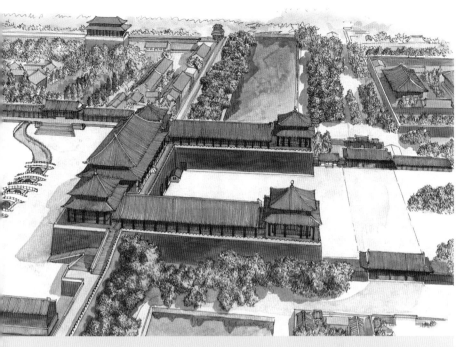

The main entrance to this courtyard, Wu Men, is an inverted U-shaped gate that faces west, north and east and is entered from the south. There are five portals into the Forbidden City through this gate. The axial entrance was for the emperor alone. His wife was allowed to use it once, on their wedding day. The other portals were for lesser dignitaries; no ordinary citizen was ever allowed in the Forbidden City.

official workshops and three lakes named North Sea, Middle Sea and South Sea. Behind the Forbidden City was a man-made mountain built from the excavated soil of the moat.

The innermost city, the Forbidden City, stood at the core of the entire project. The principal arrangement of the palace followed tradition, which was for official buildings to be located in front, and family houses to the rear, along the south-north and secondary east-west axes respectively.

The main function of the emperor's official buildings in the outer courtyard was for formal ceremonies and state occasions. Dealing with daily affairs, meeting with ministers or publishing public notices were taken care of within the inner court official buildings.

The family area then lay beyond the official area. The only virile male allowed in this area over a 590-year period was the emperor himself. The only

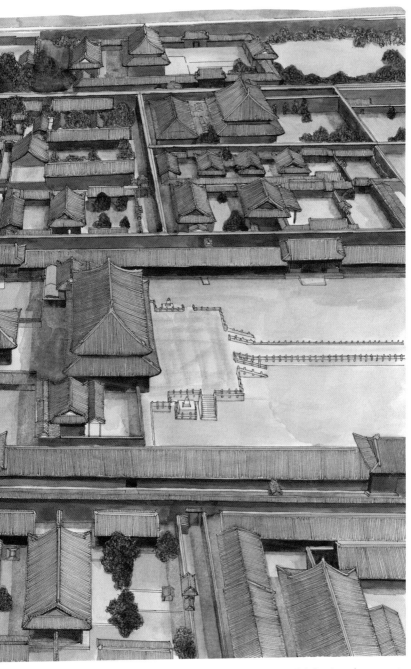

The inner palaces are miniatures of the outer ones. They were used for the daily functions of government, or sometimes, as residences.

There is a single gate in each of the four walls of the Forbidden City. At every corner of the walls is an elaborate tower displaying majestic rooflines. These are among the most beautiful structures in the entire complex, and from the towers, there is a panoramic view of Beijing and the Forbidden City.

other persons allowed in the inner court were his wife, his concubines and many eunuchs. When the emperor's sons reached the age of eight, they were sent elsewhere to live, except for crown princes.

Behind the family area along the main axis was the palace garden, a profoundly formal and solemn place. Behind the garden was the north gate, called Shen Wu Men, and then beyond that, Jingshan Park, the mountain created from excavated earth.

Although the Forbidden City is one-sixth the size of the original palace complex of the Tang dynasty (619 – 907), it is much more dense and complicated. All roofs were covered in yellow glaze tiles, except for the library in black. All walls were built of red or purple bricks filled with mortar and angled to make them strong and impenetrable. When seen against a blue sky, the effect was magnificent and awe inspiring. That this scene also inspired fear was deliberate, striving to ensure an orderly society in those times.

Imperial Tombs of the Ming Dynasty

The first emperor of the Ming dynasty, Zhu Yuanzhang, was born into a very poor family, and throughout his life retained much of the manner of his people and class. He did not have the refined sensibilities that incline one to admire gardens or other cultural pursuits. Due to this, he ordered that later generations not build gardens, so during the Ming dynasty no imperial gardens were built. However, he did feel great respect for his elders and spent lavishly on tombs for his grandparents, parents and himself.

Following his lead, future emperors spent up to one quarter of central government income on tombs. Therefore, the quality of imperial tombs after the Song (960 – 1297) and Yuan (1206 – 1368) dynasties shows marked change, some say improvement. Today we can only marvel at the extravagance and try to understand the sentiment of the time.

In the fifth year of his reign, Zhu Di's wife, Empress Xu, died. Since he did not plan to build a mausoleum in Nanjing, he sent Zhao Gong, the Minister of the Department of Ceremony, and Liao Junqing, a famous *fengshui* expert (geomancer) to look for an auspicious burial site near Beijing. Some potential site names were suitable but their pronunciation was not.

In 1409, suitable burial grounds were found about 45 kilometers north of Beijing.

An image of a general, one of the stone images at Imperial Tombs of the Ming Dynasty

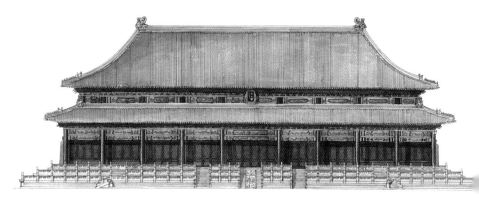

This huge hall, the Hall of Prominent Favor, is remarkable in that it is still intact. Each of its 62 camphor (*nanmu*) pillars was hewn from a single trunk of a tree grown in the far southwest of China and carried long distances to the site. Such trees no longer exist but the wood of these columns is still fragrant. The four central columns are 1.17 meters in diameter and the tallest are 14 meters. The roof has no beams and the whole chamber is lined with fine stone.

The Changling Mausoleum has its official area, consisting of three yards, in front, and the "living" area, consisting of a large round-hilled tomb, in the back. The main hall was in the second yard, 66.64 wide and 29.30 meters deep (even larger than the main hall, Taihedian, in the Forbidden City). Two accompanying halls, which have since collapsed, were on each side of the square in the front of the main hall. The tomb mounds are 266 meters south to north and 307.5 meters east to west. A wall, much like the Great Wall with fortifications and guard towers, encircles the secret location of the coffin chamber and the nearby residential areas for officials, eunuchs, guards and gardeners, who supplied sacrifice offerings, cared for, and defended the mausoleum.

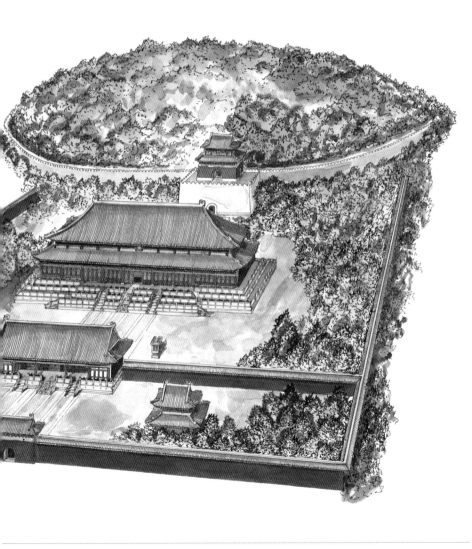

The overall design of the tomb complex was similar to that of an imperial palace, with a long south-north axial along which there are avenues, gates, squares, pavilions and chambers. An enormous memorial archway leads to an avenue 6.6 kilometers long, culminating at the coffin chamber. Along this path are a roofed gate, a large pavilion for a stone tablet, 18 sculptures of animals, ministers and generals, and a fire-pattern gate.

Forty square kilometers were set aside for the construction of the Changling Mausoleum. Zhu Di toured the site and approved of it, a beautiful valley with an excellent military perspective surrounded on three sides by mountains. The land for the entire necropolis was expropriated from the farmers living there, and for the next two hundred years commoners were forbidden.

While it was originally built for Zhu Di and his empresses alone, the succeeding twelve emperors of the Ming dynasty were also buried here. An exception is the seventh emperor, Zhu Qiyu, who attempted an unsuccessful coup d'etat of his brother. While there were many more emperors in both the Han (206 BC – AD 220) and Tang dynasties (618 – 907), they had separate tombs located far from one another. Only one dynasty in Chinese history, the Ming, can claim that their ancestors were buried in a single area.

The first and biggest tomb, Changling, at the center, was finished in 1413 and Zhu Di was buried there in 1424. Changling is located in front of the main mountain peak, which Zhu Di renamed Long Life Mountain (Tian Shou Shan).

Unlike Changling, Dingling mausoleum is completely underground. In 1956, Chinese archeologists opened Dingling, where Zhu Yijun, the thirteenth and longest-serving emperor, and his two wives were entombed. The plan takes the form of a T followed by an H. The coffin chamber of 1,195 square meters is arched in stone. It is open for visitors and over 3,000 artifacts and treasures are on display in adjacent buildings.

The Temple of Heaven

In 1420, the Ming dynasty began to set up temples to worship the God of Heaven and the God of Earth. The earliest form was a single temple devoted to both the God of Heaven and the God of Earth, but in 1530, they began to worship the God of Heaven and the God of Earth separately. In 1545, an Altar of Prayer for Good Harvest and a Hall of Prayer for Good Harvest were built for emperors to pray for favorable weather to ensure a good harvest. The Hall of Prayer for Good Harvest is the main building in the Temple of Heaven complex, and it is the highest of existing round buildings.

In 1553, a rectangular area was added to Beijing city at the northern edge of the original city walls. Thus the city walls enclosed the Temple of Heaven. The Temple of Heaven's inner walls and outer walls have the same shape: the southeastern and southwestern corners are right-angled; the northeastern and northwestern corners are round. In this way, the four corners symbolize the ancient Chinese concept of "Round Heaven and Square Earth." The distance between the east and west outer walls is 1,703 meters and the distance between the north and south outer walls is 1,657 meters. The circumference of the outer walls is 6,553 meters and the total area of the temple is 273 hectares, which is 3.7 times as large as the Forbidden City.

The Hall of Prayer for Good Harvest at the Temple of Heaven, Beijing

The Temple of Heaven has only a few buildings, the most important of which is the Circular Mound Altar (for the worship of heaven) on the south edge of the axis and the Altar of Prayer for Good Crops on the north edge. To the north of the Circular Mound Altar is a small yard enclosed by a round wall, on the north edge of which is a round hall with a pointed ceiling named the Imperial Heavenly Vault. Devoted to the Jade Emperor, the Imperial Vault was also used to perform worship ceremonies in honor of

The lower part of the Hall of Prayer for Good Harvest is a three-tiered round base made of white stones. The overall plan is a circle. The three-story Hall has a pointed roofline, which rises towards the sky. Its stunning elegance and beauty rank the Hall among one of the most charming existing ancient buildings in China.

the gods of the sun, the moon, the stars, clouds, rain, wind and thunder.

Between the Imperial Vault and the Hall of Prayer for Good Harvest is an elevated road that is 361.3 meters in length and 29.4 meters in width. Although the road remains horizontally, at the Imperial Vault it is only a little bit higher than ground level, while the other end it is 3.35 meters higher than the ground. This is because the land in the Temple of Heaven is a north-facing slope.

CHAPTER 8

THE QING DYNASTY

Xuguang Pavilion at Pule Temple, one of the Eight Outlying Temples, Hebei Province

Although a time of architectural and artistic achievements, the Ming dynasty (1368 – 1644) was also one of the darkest eras in Chinese political history. After the foundation of Ming dynasty, the first emperor Zhu Yuanzhang began to slaughter the people to whom he owed much, as he feared that these people might jeopardize his throne. Then, after Zhu Di captured Nanjing, he slaughtered the relatives of former court officials. The Ming dynasty also witnessed the invention of brutal methods of torture and the relentless executions of many people who suffered from injustice. It can be said that there was little justice during the duration of the Ming dynasty, leading to its eventual fall.

After well over two centuries of rule, the Ming dynasty was overthrown by a rebel army led by Li Zicheng. He, in turn, was swiftly defeated by the army of the Manchu, one of the Chinese ethnic minorities living in the north. Although a nomadic nationality with a small population, the Manchu army was able to rule China, establishing the Qing dynasty (1644 – 1911), which lasted for well over two hundred years.

Fortunately, the Forbidden City was not destroyed during its capture by either the rebel army led by Li Zicheng or the Manchu army. To the Manchu people, who had been used to living in tents, the Forbidden City

Jichang Garden, Wuxi, Jiangsu Province, is a paragon among private gardens in southern China. Emperor Kangxi and Emperor Qianlong, two of the most famous emperors of the Qing dynasty, each made six royal visits here, and this garden served as a model for their royal gardens in Chengde and Beijing.

was a heaven-like place. The Qing left intact much of the Ming dynasty architecture, including the Forbidden City and temples in Beijing. They did not build other imperial palaces. Therefore, the architectural achievement of the Qing dynasty is mainly reflected in its imperial gardens and the Eight Outlying Temples of Chengde.

In China, private gardens emerged after royal gardens. From the Han dynasty to the era of the Wei, Jin, Northern and Southern dynasties (206 BC – AD 589), the Chinese people experienced much political turmoil and social chaos. As a result, Confucianism gave way to Taoism. Many intellectuals found shelter among mountains in order to stay away from wars. Moderation and metaphysics became a fashion of scholars and officials. This nature-loving philosophy contributed to the development of Chinese landscape painting and private gardens. Early gardens in the idyllic landscapes of small, remote villages later evolved into the gardens of mansions in towns and cities.

The heyday of private gardens was in the Qing dynasty. The major private gardens were mainly distributed in the southern areas of the lower reaches of the Yangtze River, including Suzhou, Yangzhou and Wuxi, among

Jichang Garden, Wuxi, Jiangsu Province, is a typical example among private gardens in southern Jiangsu Province. For four hundred years following its completion, the garden was in the possession of the Qin Family, until 1949, when it was nationalized by the People's Republic of China.

other cities. The largest private garden had an area of 4.2 hectares while the smallest had an area of no more than 200 square meters.

The owners were mainly wealthy people of literary and artistic refinement. Garden designers took as their inspiration the imagery of Chinese landscape paintings. The artists artfully divided space into different layers. Doors, windows, brick walls with openwork, and corridors were some of the features used so that scenes opened onto one another, screened and only partially revealed, with elegant vagueness.

Artificial hills and small water features were vital to these gardens, representing real mountains and bodies of water. Designers often bestowed the gardens with a name bearing cultural allusions, sometimes moralistic or self-mocking. The visual and cultural allusions led visitors into a universe of imagination. Therefore, gardens resemble Chinese landscape paintings, in that both are the combination of imagination and visual images.

Chengde Summer Resort

Chengde Summer Resort

Chengde Summer Resort was the first imperial garden built in the Qing dynasty. The construction was inaugurated in 1703, 42 years after Emperor Kangxi was enthroned, and took many years to complete. Since the Manchus were nomadic, after they came to power, the royal family maintained the tradition of hunting on the grassland in the north every autumn and migrating to resorts in the sweltering heat of summer.

A picturesque village with mountains and water, Chengde is a pleasant resort to the northeast of Beijing. In Chengde, there are summer palaces of emperors as well as a hot spring called Rehe (meaning "hot river"). In winter, the river next to the hot spring does not freeze. In summer, the river water feels refreshingly cool. The Summer Resort was modeled after the gardens in the southern areas at the lower reaches of the Yangtze River, which impressed Emperor Kangxi during his six trips to Wuxi, a southern city famous for gardening.

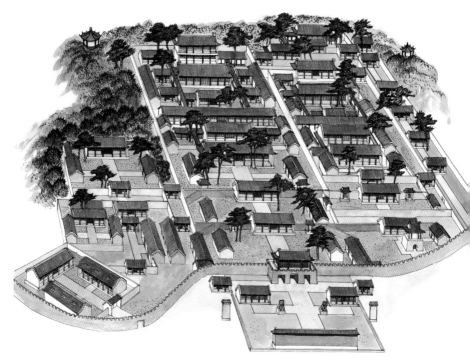

The Summer Resort is comprised of a palace area, shown here, and a garden area. It served as the second imperial palace, because emperors would spend half a year here performing ceremonies and conducting official business. The large garden area contains mountains, plains and lakes. With a total area of 564 hectares, the Summer Resort is the largest existing royal garden.

The construction of the Summer Resort also had a political purpose, i.e. receiving the homage visits by the leaders of ethnic minorities. Good relations with ethnic minorities, who mostly lived in remote border areas, bore great significance to border security. However, the leaders of the Mongolians and other ethnic minorities were reluctant to go to the populous Beijing City, fearful that they might contract the deadly disease of small pox. So a summer palace in Chengde, where there were few people, served as a place where the emperor could more easily converse with leaders from ethnic minorities.

The heart of the Summer Resort is found in the 57-hectare lake area. There used to be nine lakes and ten islands, while now there are seven lakes and eight islands. More than half of the buildings of the resort are located here.

As a royal garden, the Summer Resort has unique characteristics. The resort was built on the basis of local topography, without digging earth to make lakes or heaping earth into hills. The overall style is natural but elegant, quite in tune with the northern scenery beloved by the Manchus. The architecture in the Summer Resort was also influenced by scenery in other parts of China. Therefore, the Summer Resort can be seen as a perfect miniature of the greater Chinese artistic treasure. However, instead of merely copying from models, the Chengde Summer instead pursues a substantial resemblance in essence. The design of the royal garden is of unequaled elegance and refinement.

Summer Palace and Old Summer Palace

Located in the western suburb of Beijing, the Old Summer Palace (Yuanming Yuan) was finished in 1744, with an area of 347 hectares. Although not as large as the Chengde Summer Resort, the Old Summer Palace had much better architecture as well as a rich collection of cultural relics in almost every hall or house. These included drawings and calligraphy that had been passed down from ancient times, preserved by royal families of the Ming dynasty or offered as tributes. Unfortunately, this garden was plundered and burnt by the invading Anglo-French allied forces in

Remnants of Xiyang Lou, literally "western mansions", a building at the Old Summer Palace

As a picturesque scenic spot in the Old Summer Palace, this hall, laid on a white stone foundation, appears splendid and elegant. It displays majesty suited to architecture in an imperial garden.

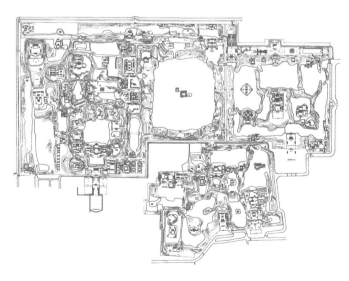

General plan of Old Summer Palace

The Summer Palace was the last Chinese royal garden, and therefore, it is the best in many ways. Its location is almost perfect and it shows superb design. Viewed from downtown Beijing, the garden has West Mountain as its background. At the garden's center, there is a natural lake, in which the West Mountain casts its shadow. When expanding the lake, the craftsmen used the excavated earth to heighten Longevity Hill.

1860. A substantial part of the cultural relics were destroyed or ransacked by the invaders.

The Summer Palace (Yihe Yuan) was reconstructed in 1886, and among the existing royal gardens, it is the one with the highest artistic level. It was built under the Empress Dowager, whom almost all Chinese people had come to loathe due to her manipulation of the royal court. In view of this fact, it was said that Empress Dowager embezzled the funds from the navy in order to construct the Summer Palace for herself.

The palace area is located in the northeast corner of the garden, and includes the administrative area and residence of the Empress Dowager. The buildings are not symmetrically distributed along the axis; instead the scenic

Buddhist temples were a necessary part of royal gardens built in Qing dynasty. The Buddhist temple in the Summer Palace is located on the southern slope of Longevity Hill. The axis of the temple is symmetrical and its front is lower than its back.

This three-story building in the Garden of Harmonious Virtue in Summer Palace was where the Empress Dowager could entertain herself by watching opera performances at any time.

spots and buildings are arranged with arbitrariness and elegance. The Hall of Longevity in Happiness is where the Empress Dowager used to live. The lake in front of the Hall of Longevity in Happiness and the hill behind the hall constitute a pleasant scene.

The lake scenery in the Summer Palace was modeled after the West Lake of Hangzhou, a famous scenic spot in China. The western bank divides the lake into inner lake, outer lake and northwestern waters. Three large islands were arranged, the design of which, as we have seen, has its origin in the Western Han dynasty, based on the legend of the Fairy Mountain and the elixir of immortality pursued by Qin Shi Huang, the First Emperor.

The scenic spots in the Summer Palace are concentrated, with one following another. These include the lofty Longevity Hill; Kunming Lake, which is the largest body of water in Chinese royal gardens; the Long Gallery,

Behind Longevity Hill, there are Tibetan-style religious buildings along the slope. Underneath is Houxi River (Rear River), along the banks of which there are two stretches of marketplace called "Maimaijie" (meaning "business street"). The emperor of that time envied the "carefree" life of common people, and this artificial business street was thus constructed so he could enjoy himself by shopping together with concubines, with eunuchs serving as shopkeepers.

which is the longest gallery in China; and the Garden of Harmonious Interest, a delicate garden inside a larger garden. Therefore, there is no doubt that the Summer Palace ranks highest among Chinese gardens.

The Eight Outlying Temples

Besides royal gardens, the Eight Outlying Temples in Chengde are the most noteworthy architectural achievement of the Qing dynasty. Tibetan Buddhism, which emerged in the Yuan dynasty, was also the religion of the royal family of the Qing dynasty. The Qing government understood the value of appeasing ethnic minorities such as Tibetans and Mongolians by promoting Tibetan Buddhism. It was a consistent policy of the Qing to construct and provide for important lamaseries using royal taxes.

The Qing Government provided for 40 lamaseries, more than 30 of which are located in Beijing and eight of which are located in Chengde. As Chengde lies to the north of the Great Wall, people usually call these eight lamaseries the Eight Outlying Temples. Actually, there used to be twelve lamaseries in Chengde. However, since the royal family initially provided financial support to eight lamaseries, people were used to the name of Eight Outlying Temples, and the name was kept until today, although there have been changes to the number.

Great importance is attached to the architecture of the Eight Outlying Temples because their design broke away from the fixed mainstream tradition in China at that time and brought forth a fresh appearance. The Eight Outlying Temples exhibit the most innovative architectural design of the Qing dynasty, apart from garden design. A new breath of life was thus blown into the already stagnant Chinese architectural art.

Among the Eight Outlying Temples, Putuozongcheng Lamasery, Xumifushou Lamasery, Puning Temple and Pule Temple have the most striking design.

Adopting Tibetan architectural style was one of the innovative measures of the Eight Outlying Temples. The design of Putuozongcheng Lamasery, the largest among the Eight Outlying Temples, is modeled on that of the Potala Palace in Lhasa. The main body of Putuozongcheng Lamasery is comprised of the Grand Vermilion Terrace at the back of the architectural complex,

The ceiling of the Wanfaguiyi Hall, the main building of the Putuozongcheng Lamasery, one of the Eight Outlying Temples in Chengde, Hebei Province

Dacheng Pavilion at Puning Temple, one of the Eight Outlying Temples

which has a height of 43 meters and an area of 10,000 square meters.

Just like the Jichang Garden, also located on a mountain, the base of the Grand Vermilion Terrace is settled on the mountain and then extends up, covering the part of mountain with protection walls that form part of the Terrace's exterior. The building looks higher than it is, with a solid part of the mountain inside the protection walls. Viewed from its exterior, it is an encircled Tibetan building, while viewed from its interior, it is a square hall surrounded by three-storied corridors. The square hall in the center has a magnificent pyramid roof with gold-plated copper edges.

Like Putuozongcheng Lamasery, Xumifushou Lamasery is a Buddhist temple featuring Tibetan architecture. As the last temple to be built in Chengde by the Qing government, it synthesized many merits of other temples, with delicate and appropriate spatial design.

Xumifushou Lamasery also has its main construction a Grand Vermilion

A glazed memorial arch at the Xumifushou Lamasery, one of the Eight Outlying Temples, Chengde, Hebei Province

Terrace on the rear edge of its axis. The main hall surrounded by the encircling building has three stories and a double-eave pyramid roof with gold-plated copper edges. On each of the four roof ridges, there are two gold-plated copper dragons. Vivid and large, each of the dragons weighs more than one ton. This is a rare perfect combination of sculptural and architectural sophistication.

Behind the Grand Vermilion Terrace, there is a seven-storied glazed pagoda, which is an octagon in plan. This colorful pagoda is one of the symbols of the temple, because it is located in the temple's highest point and adds distinctiveness to the temple.

Among the Eight Outlying Temples, Puning Temple attracts the most tourist visits, because of its huge statue of Avalokitesvara Bodhisattva in Dacheng Hall. As the main hall of the temple, Dacheng Hall is located in the center of the complex and represents the Mount Sumeru, the center of Buddhist universe. On the two sides are the Hall of the Sun and the Hall of the Moon. Around Dacheng Hall, there are halls of different shapes in the east, west, south and north, representing the major elements of earth, water, fire and wind. Further off are eight two-storied white platforms representing the eight minor elements. On the four corners of the hall, there are four gourd-shaped Tibetan pagodas representing the four wisdoms of Buddha. The complex architectural design is a vivid representation of the Buddhist world.

Pule Temple is another impressive architectural group. Pule Temple is dubbed "the round pavilion," because Xuguang Pavilion, its main architectural feature looks like the Temple of Heaven, except for its two-storied roof. However, on a close inspection, there are major differences with the Temple of Heaven. The base of Xuguang Pavilion is a three-storied

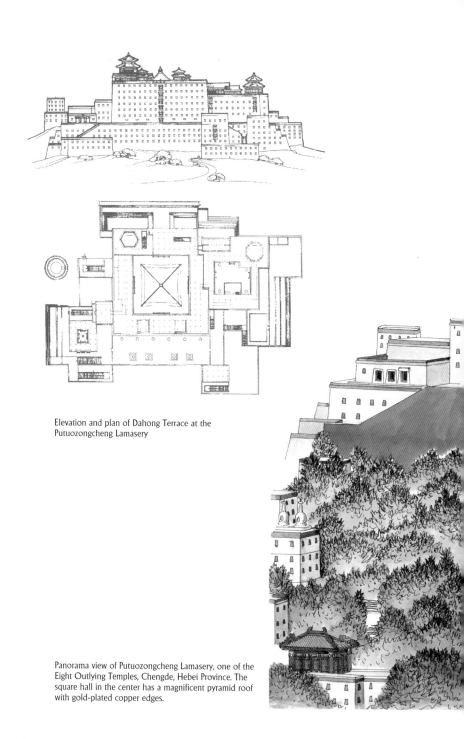

Elevation and plan of Dahong Terrace at the
Putuozongcheng Lamasery

Panorama view of Putuozongcheng Lamasery, one of the
Eight Outlying Temples, Chengde, Hebei Province. The
square hall in the center has a magnificent pyramid roof
with gold-plated copper edges.

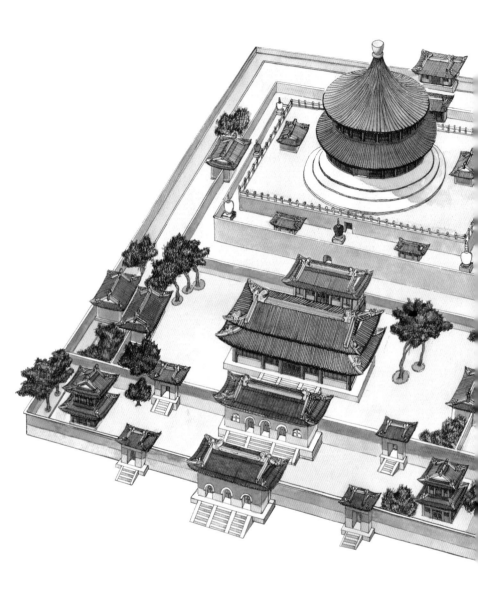

Pule Temple, one of the Eight Outlying Temples in Hebei Province, combines both Han and Tibetan architectural styles. The front is in the Han style, while the rear of the temple is Tibetan.

square base with four identical facades and a door centered on each side. On the second floor, there are eight gourd-shaped Tibetan pagodas set symmetrically on the four corners and the center of each facade. The eight pagodas have different colors and stand for the eight accomplishments of Sakyamuni. In the center of the uppermost floor there is a copper Buddha statue depicting a man and a woman copulating while looking each other in the eye. The statue, known as Jolly Buddha, represents the highest practice level according to the esoteric branch of Tibetan Buddhism.

In summary, the Eight Outlying Temples integrate rich imagination, vigor and artistic value. They are particularly noteworthy, given the fact that they were created in the Qing dynasty, when there was a lack of innovation and a prevalence of stagnant design. The Eight Outlying Temples stand out as a treasure of Chinese architectural history.

The Potala Palace

After discussing the Eight Outlying Temples in Chengde, it is natural to think of their prototype, the Potala Palace. Located on the Putuo Mountain in the center of Lhasa, the Potala Palace was built in the era of King Songtsen Gampo (7th century). In 1645, the Fifth Dalai Lama decided to reconstruct the Potala Palace, which had been severely damaged by that time. The reconstruction lasted 50 years. The palace, with an area of more than 40 hectares, served as both a temple and a palace where the Dalai Lamas lived, undertook official work and performed Buddhist ceremonies.

The fortress-style palace was built upwards from the mountainside. Viewed from the outside, the palace can be divided into the Red Palace and

Although the main body of the Red Palace at the Potala Palace is in the Tibetan style, seven large roofs in the Han style were built on the flat top. With their gold-plated tiles, the roofs look gorgeous.

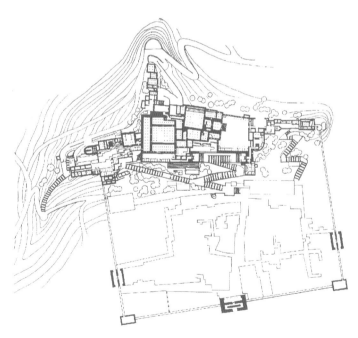

General plan of Potala Palace, with an area of more than 40 hectares, where the Dalai Lamas used to live, undertake official duties, and perform Buddhist ceremonies

The Potala Palace in Lhasa, Tibet, plays a double role of palace and temple. The whole building seems to have emerged from the mountain, with a majestic, sacred and artistic air.

White Palace. The White Palace used to be the Dalai Lamas' living quarters and office area. The Red Palace served as living quarters for the monks, and for this reason, has smaller rooms. The Red Palace is located in the center of the mountain. The tops of the Tibetan-styled buildings in the Red Palace have seven Han-style roofs covered by glittering gold-plated tiles.

East Joy Square and West Joy Square are on the roof of the White Palace, in the east and west sides of the Potala Palace. West Joy Square is located right below the upper part of the Red Palace, where gigantic Buddha portraits are located. Under the West Joy Square there are nine lower stories of the Red Palace. Viewed from distance, the four windowed upper stories and the nine windowed lower stories on the façade appear to constitute a magnificent 13-storied building.

The Potala Palace was built in accordance with the topography of the mountain. The lower protection walls and the many staircases almost clothe the whole mountain. The Potala Palace has an upward tapering appearance. The building seems to have emerged from within the mountain, with a majestic, sacred and artistic air.

Jichang Garden

Jichang Garden, Wuxi, Jiangsu Province, is a jewel among private gardens in southern China.

With an area of 10,000 square meters, Jichang Garden in Wuxi is among the oldest and best-preserved classical gardens in the lower reaches of the Yangtze River. It was built in Zhengde Era (1506 – 1520) of the Ming dynasty. However, it reached its most impressive form in the Qing dynasty, under the famed garden designer Zhang Liang and his nephew Zhang Lian. In the four hundred years following its completion, the garden had been in the possession of the Qin family until 1949, when it was nationalized by the People's Republic of China.

Emperor Kangxi and Emperor Qianlong, two of the most famous emperors of the Qing dynasty, each had six royal visits south. They had their subordinates draw sketches so that the garden's features could be imitated in the construction of royal gardens in Chengde and Beijing. Nowadays, Jichang Garden is still one of the best gardens in the lower Yangtze River area.

The Humble Administrator's Garden (Zhuozheng Garden)

Suzhou now stands as the most famous garden city, boasting the largest collection of private gardens in China. The Humble Administrator's Garden is the largest existing garden in Suzhou, and also one of the best-designed

The central scenic area of the Humble Administrator's Garden (Zhuozheng Garden), Suzhou, Jiangsu Province, is the high point of the entire garden.

gardens in China. Its construction was started in the beginning of the 16th century. During the Qing dynasty, the garden saw numerous changes of owners, and the appearance of the garden today most closely resembles its late Qing appearance.

The existing part of the Humble Administrator's Garden comprises three gardens, with the central part being the best. The eastern and western parts of the garden are separated by a long corridor. The central part and the western part each have ponds at their center. There are islands dotting the ponds, which are separated into sections of different sizes by bridges that connect the islands and the bank. The buildings in the central and western part are densely distributed, forming many scene groups, many of which are near water. The buildings and the water play off one another in many ways. People can see water scenes through windows, doors and corridors. Many scene groups have elements such as artificial hills, bridges and small yards, creating a diversity of space.

Ge Garden

Located on the north bank of the Yangtze River, Yangzhou is of great geographical importance because it is the converging point of the Yangtze River and the Beijing-Hangzhou Canal. During the Qing dynasty, Yangzhou was the most important hub for salt transportation. The salt industry was an important part of revenue for the Qing dynasty.

The wealth of salt merchants was such that they could afford to make superb gardens. Huang Yingtai, a salt tycoon, built a garden featuring bamboos behind his mansion. The garden was named Ge Garden; the character for *ge* (个) is shaped like bamboo leaves and has a humorous association. Ancient Chinese intellectuals liked bamboos, which had many

The Mountain Embracing Building in Ge Garden is the largest existing hall to be found in a private garden in Yangzhou.

symbolic associations. The hollow stems stand for the modesty of people, while their straight shape stands for the personal integrity of intellectuals, who would not try to please the powerful. The bamboo canes symbolize the owner's aspirations and wishes for the future.

Ge Garden has four artificial hills, namely Spring Hill, Summer Hill, Autumn Hill and Winter Hill, as its main design elements. Each invokes its corresponding season, impressing visitors profoundly. For example, the Winter Hill is amassed using a type of rock with a white surface, giving a snow-covered appearance. The brick pavement has cracks in the shape of ice, standing for winter. In the high walls behind the hill, there are 24 round windows, beyond which there is a long corridor. The temperature gap between the two sides of the corridor generates perennial breeze that whistles through the windows. It is a vivid imitation of wintry winds.

The exaggerated artistic style in Ge Garden was obviously influenced by traditional Chinese poems and paintings. This kind of daring infusion of many romantic and artistic elements made garden design the discipline with the highest artistic value in traditional Chinese architecture. Moreover, the design of gardens involved the direct participation of intellectuals and painters, who gave garden design more individuality and personal artistic expression. Garden design also featured many variations, contrasting with Chinese Buddhist temples, which have an almost uniform layout.

At Shihu Garden, Weifang, Shandong Province, the pool, along with the bridges, pavilions and other buildings that surround it, are well integrated, demonstrating the grace and distinctiveness of gardens of Jiangnan (south of the Yangtze River).

Shihu Garden

Besides the elegant and beautiful gardens in the lower reaches of the Yangtze River, representing the Jiangnan style, Chinese private garden styles also include the North and Lingnan (south of the Five Ridges, area covering Guangdong and Guangxi Provinces) Gardens. North Gardens, as expected, are mainly scattered in northern China including Beijing, Hebei, Shanxi and Shandong. As there are more officials in the northern area, the design of North Gardens mirrors the character of official buildings under the influence of Beijing royal architecture.

Shihu Garden is a small private garden integrating the features of both northern and southern gardens. It is located in Weifang City of Shandong Province, at what used to be a residence of Hu Bangzuo, the Minister of Punishment of the Jiajin period in the Ming dynasty (1522 – 1567). In the Qing dynasty (1885), a rich gentleman, Ding Shanbao, bought it at a high cost and transformed it into a private garden.

In ancient China, the hu was a long thin tablet held by the ministers at court meetings, on which to record the emperor's orders. Chinese people regard modesty as a moral virtue, and the garden was named "Shihu" (alluding to the size of ten *hu*) to denote that the garden is very small.

In spite of its small size, the scenery shows great variety. Shihu Garden has a pond as its center, with bridges and pavilions along it. The architecture in the garden differs from that in southern gardens, which is characterized by white walls and black tiles. The buildings take red and green as the main color with the roofs covered with grey tiles, looking proper and elegant.

Lingnan Gardens

Lingnan Gardens broadly refer to those in such areas as Guangdong and Guangxi, and their history can be traced back to the Han dynasty. At the beginning of the Qing dynasty, the Pearl River Delta was relatively developed economically, so culture also flourished. The building of private gardens began to rise there and gradually influenced such areas as Chaozhou, Shantou, Fujian and Taiwan. The Lingnan style became increasingly popular from the middle period of Qing dynasty, gradually developing distinctive features in terms of patterning, layout, utilization of water and stone, and arrangement of flowers and trees.

The Lingnan area's climate, a result to its southern location and

Interior decoration at the Yuyin Villa, Panyu, Guangdong Province

The Ke Pavilion in Ke Garden, Dongguan, Guangdong Province

proximity to the South Sea, influenced the style of garden design. The plants are mostly tall and dense due to the hot and humid climate, and provide a large stretch of shadow. Compared with other Chinese gardens, Lingnan Gardens rarely use artificial hills, relying instead on colorful plant landscapes to provide vigor and interest. The area of the garden is limited, and to obtain the effect of seeing large elements from small, the courtyards use visual trickery, combining and screening spaces. This diversity demonstrates the ability of the garden design to take full advantage of a small scope and limited space.

Ke (meaning "fit") Garden in Dongguan of Guangdong province is one such example. The garden is divided into two parts: Ke Lake and Courtyard. The Courtyard, in particular, captures the essence of the garden. The three groups of buildings are arranged irregularly, surrounded by a long lane, showing inventiveness and spontaneity.

Since Lingnan is a coastal area, it was exposed to foreign culture. Its gardens show the influence of native culture from central China integrated with overseas culture, and therefore, Lingnan Gardens demonstrate some of the features of Western classical gardens. As an example, the biggest feature of Yuyinshanfang Garden is its symmetrical geometric patterning, which greatly contrasts with traditional Chinese gardens characterized by a free and varied patterning.

The memorial archway at the Qingdongling of the Qing dynasty

Royal Tombs of Qing Dynasty

There are six royal tombs of the Qing dynasty. These include four "outside the pass," i.e. in the area beyond the mountain pass where the Manchus entered to occupy the south of the Great Wall. These are in Liaoling, and emperors and their ancestors from before the time the Qing entered the pass were buried there. The other two royal tombs were Qingdongling and Qingxiling in Hebei Province, where the nine emperors of the Qing dynasty and their queens and concubines, along with princes and princesses, were buried. These two are the most important and typical of Qing dynasty tombs.

Qingdongling is located on Changrui Mountain in Malanyu of Zunhua County. The earliest royal tomb built after the Qing entered central China, it is also the largest and most well-preserved among existing Qing dynasty royal tombs. There are altogether five royal tombs in the complex, as well as over twelve for queens, concubines, princesses and princes.

The tomb architecture clearly demonstrates the rank of the deceased. The emperor's tomb has the most complete system and largest scale, next is the queen's,

then the others arranged according to their rank and status. According to Qing custom, after the emperor died, he was buried in an underground palace and the door of the tomb was permanently sealed. Therefore, if the queen died after the emperor, another tomb needed to be built. No independent queen's tomb was built before the Qing dynasty. In Qingdongling, there are not only queen's tombs but also those of the concubines. Thus, the Qing dynasty left the richest royal tomb system.

The general layout of Qingdongling is similar to the Ming Tombs, both characterized by using the earliest emperor's tomb as the center, with other tombs lined up on both sides and a mountain as a barrier behind each of the emperors' tombs. There is a long central axis, starting from Jinxingshan Mountain, then passing Shipailou Building, Dahongmen Gate, Dapailou Building through to Xiao Tomb, where Emperor Shunzhi (reign: 1644 –

The stone images of Jingling Tomb for Emperor Kangxi, at the Dongling Mausoleum of the Qing dynasty

1660) was buried. The axis provides a focal point, bringing all of the red-walled, yellow-tiled buildings scattered among the forest under the solemn atmosphere of the tomb zone.

The building system in the Qingdongling area basically follows that of the Ming Tombs in terms of layout, structure and scale, but shows improvement in some details. So far, only Yu Tomb's underground palace, where Emperor Qianlong (reign: 1736 – 1795) was buried, has been opened. Here, delicate Buddhas were sculpted on the stone gate and walls of the palace, giving us some sense of the overall artistic refinement of the tomb complex.

The Ding Tomb in the east, or Dingdongling, is a tomb for the two queens, Cixi and Ci'an. Queen Ci'an married Emperor Xianfeng before he was enthroned and was honored as Queen when he became emperor. After

The Dongling Mausoleum's Dingdong Tomb, for the Empress Dowageres Cixi and Ci'an

Xianfeng died, Zaichun, the son of the concubine Yiguifei, was placed on the throne since Queen Ci'an did not have a son. Thus Yiguifei was respected as Queen Cixi. Ci'an was called the East Queen as she lived in the Zhongcui Palace on the east road of the Forbidden City, while Cixi was called the West Queen as she lived in the Chuxiu Palace on the west road. After Emperor Xianfeng died, Cixi and Ci'an jointly helped with the emperor's rule.

Dingdongling is very special in that the two tombs are built on the same side with a trench in between. They were built and completed at the same time. However, after Cixi monopolized power, she rebuilt the tomb to make it more luxurious. A lot of precious materials such as nanmu wood and rosewood were used and the decoration was more magnificent and delicate. Gilding was added to the paintings, and dragons and phoenixes engraved on the head of balusters, making Dingdongling the highest in terms of artistic standard among the numerous queens' tombs of the Qing dynasty.

Qingxiling, in Yi County of Hebei Province, is also one of the most important tombs of the Qing dynasty. It was first built during Yongzheng period (reign: 1723 – 1735). Its general scale and building system are similar to those of Qingdongling.

Confucius Temples

Early in the Han dynasty (206 BC – AD 220), Confucianism became the orthodox thought of the Chinese feudal society. At many points during the many centuries of feudal society, Confucian classics were the highest creed of the ruling class. Many were preserved over the years, and form a rich national cultural heritage.

To talk about Confucianism, one has to mention its founder. Known in the west as Confucius (551 – 479 BC), and named Kongqiu, called Zhongni,

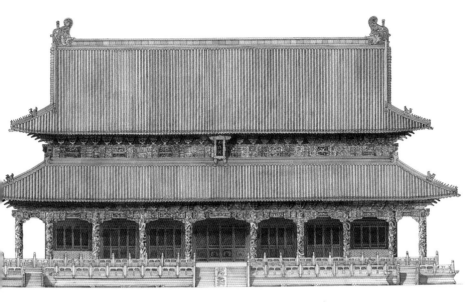

Front elevation of Dacheng Hall, Confucius Temple, with its magnificent dragon columns

he is China's greatest educator and thinker. He has been respected by later generations as the "Extreme Saint" (the saint among the saints), and his thoughts and doctrines have had an extremely far-reaching effect.

The cornerstone of Confucianism, the Analects, was compiled by the disciples of Confucius and their disciples. It records the words and acts of Confucius and his disciples. Confucianism has been passed on through written and oral means, and has an architectural legacy as well, through the building of temples. Confucius' hometown, Qufu in Shandong Province, is the focus for the building of Confucius temples. Unfortunately, due to fires and other reasons, the current buildings in Qufu mainly only date back to the Ming and Qing dynasties.

Confucius temples follow the standard plan of using central axes, with the building sitting on the north and facing the south. At the Confucius Temple in Qufu, from south to north, there are eight courtyards. The first three courtyards set the stage for the whole space, with green pine trees creating a solemn atmosphere, demonstrating quiet and vigor. After passing

Confucius Temple in Qufu

through the big middle gate, there is the main building of the Confucius temple. Its main body imitates a palace with a surrounding courtyard wall with turrets built on the four corners. From the big gate, leading into the sixth courtyard, is the central building of Confucius temple, i.e. Dacheng Hall, and next is the bedroom of the wife of Confucius.

Dacheng Hall was first built in the Song dynasty (960 – 1279) and rebuilt during the Yongzheng period of the Qing dynasty. The hall opens wide to nine rooms with saddle roofs and heavy eaves. On the roof top are yellow glazed tiles. The ten columns in the front eave are all carved of stone, their bodies fully decorated with reliefs showing flying dragons playing with a ball, showing the superior skills of the sculptors.

Dacheng Hall and the bedroom hall follow the model of front hall and back bedroom that can otherwise only be seen in royal architecture. This is a rare example of Chinese ancient architecture that combines the style of royal architecture with religious elements. Along with royal and religious features, due to the nature of Confucius's character, some features of academic and educational architecture also appear.

Guozijian

The highest institute of learning in China's traditional education system was the Guozixue, later called Guozijian. The Guozixue was set up in 278, and then demolished while the Taixue was established. After Emperor Yang of Sui dynasty (reign: 605 – 618) came to power, it was changed to Guozijian. The Guozijian in the Qing dynasty was in charge of all kinds of official learning in the country. The Beijing Guozijian, which existed under the Yuan, Ming and Qing dynasties, is located on Guozijian Street in the Dongcheng District of Beijing. It is the last Guozijian in China.

The Beijing Guozijian is divided into two parts: Taixue (central government school) and Confucius Temple. The Confucius Temple is located on the left side of the Taixue, following the ancient system of left side for temple and right side for learning. The central building of the Taixue is Piyong, a type of structure that dates back to the Western Zhou dynasty (1046 – 771 BC). After the Eastern Han dynasty (25 – 220), there were Piyongs for generations, all for paying tribute.

The Piyong of the Beijing Guozijian was built in the 49th year of Qianlong of the Qing dynasty (1784). It is a square-shape hall built on a square stone platform with heavy eaves and a four-angle pyramidal roof. Around the hall is a pond, known as "Round Pond." The combination of the round pond and square hall complies with the ancient concept of "Round Heaven and Square Earth." Piyong Hall opens its gates on four sides, connecting with the four bridges over the round pond and the pond bank. Seen from afar, the yellow-tile and red-column square hall is like a palace floating on the river.

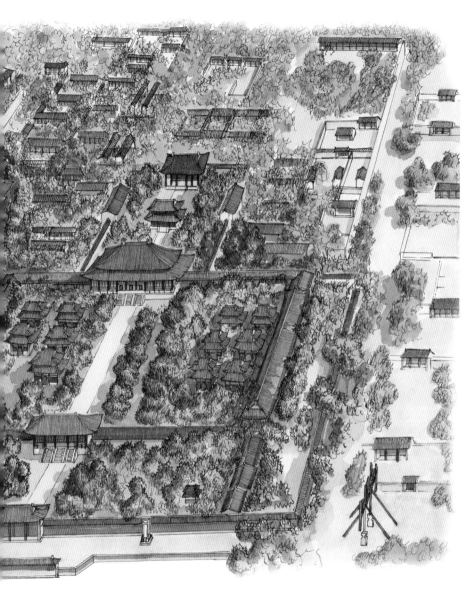

Panorama view of Guozijian, Beijing, the highest institute of learning in Chinese feudal times

CHAPTER 9
CHINESE DOMESTIC ARCHITECTURE

A ncient Chinese architecture roughly falls into two types: official and folk or domestic. Official buildings mainly included palaces and government offices; altars and temples; mausoleums; and mansions. Folk buildings consist primarily of residential dwellings, but also include ancestral temples, gates to stockaded villages, bridges and opera platforms. The most notable feature about Chinese folk architecture is that it was tailor-made to its location and situation. This architecture took different forms based on the widely varying natural conditions such as geography and climate. People adapted to these conditions to create a suitable residential form. In some cases, these traditions continue to the present day.

From a broad perspective, unlike imperial buildings, which were severely restricted and restrained by the customs, rituals and regulations of the over two-thousand-year-old feudal system, Chinese folk buildings were flexible. However, their creation was not totally free; restrictions were placed by the feudal social ranking system of the time as well as factors such as folk customs and habits, and geography and environment. The accumulation of experience of generation after generation has led to a rich tradition of domestic architecture, which, with artistry and charm, represents the characteristics of its respective region.

Courtyard Houses

Courtyard houses, with their combination of structure and adaptability, are the most prevalent residential mode of Chinese folk housing. They have a long history and geographic distribution. Courtyard folk houses are

The screen gate inside the Hanging Flower Gate of traditional courtyard houses in Beijing

scattered throughout China, ranging from the standard courtyard houses in northeastern China and the quadrangle dwellings in Beijing and central Shanxi Province to the Bai nationality folk houses in Dali and the Naxi nationality folk houses in Lijiang of Yunnan Province.

The courtyard folk houses in central Shanxi Province usually consist of several compounds, and these relatively big courtyards were often built for rich merchants. These courtyards were mostly built of brick, and their big and tall walls provide very good defense, which may be due to the fact that most of the able men went out on business, leaving the old and weak, and women and children at home.

Although these courtyards look simple, the interiors were decorated extremely luxuriously to demonstrate the owners' status. Since they were far from the capital city, the decorations were less restricted. For example, in the area of the capital, corbel brackets were only allowed to be used for official buildings; they do appear in some Shanxi houses, however.

The parvis-style folk house was the main form of courtyard residential house in southern China. In this style, houses connect on the four sides at the corners of the compounds, leaving an open free space in the center of the courtyard, looking like a well seen from above. Among this type of courtyard folk houses, the quadrangle courtyard in Beijing is the most typical. Its use dates to the early Yuan dynasty (1279 – 1368).

Simply speaking, the quadrangle courtyard in Beijing is a kind of compound formed by connecting up the houses on four sides. The courtyard is square with a proportional size. A veranda is typically used to connect the houses. The outer wall of the compound seldom contains windows, providing secure privacy, while the inside is spacious and defined.

The layout of the quadrangle courtyard reflects China's ancient patriarchal clan and rite systems, and therefore it is organized according to complex rules incomparable to the folk houses in other areas. The room arrangement reflects the status of the different household members, in hierarchy as to seniority, gender and role. For example, the principal house located on the northern side of the courtyard is the largest and the most important one. The central room of the principal house is where the household ancestral hall is located, housing the ancestors' memorial tablets.

The rooms on the eastern and western sides of the principal house were inhabited by grandparents and parents. Wing-rooms built in front of the principal house on the eastern side usually housed the eldest and third son while second son and fourth son lived on the western side. Daughters of the household master lived in the rear room located at the back of the compound. This was the area with the strongest privacy from the outside world, and since daughters need to pass through the parents' principal house, it was easy

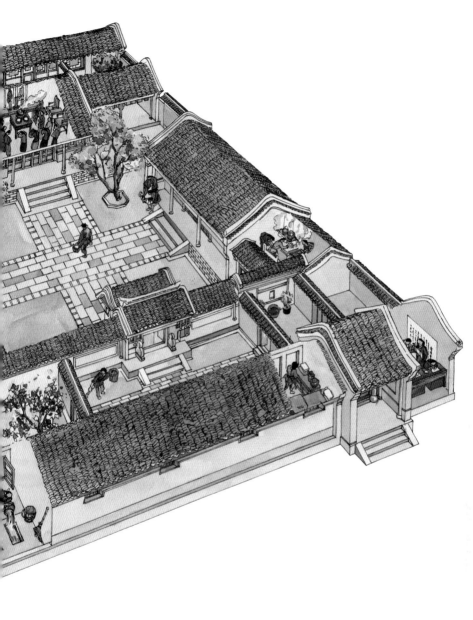

Sectional and perspective view of traditional courtyards in Beijing

The magnificent central gate is called Hanging Flower Gate

The screen wall in traditional courtyard houses

for parents to monitor their actions.

While there are many kinds of gates for the quadrangle courtyard in Beijing, there are five most common ones. The kind of gate used was determined by social status. The gates used Beijing have a very high

The drum-shaped stone in front of the gate of traditional courtyard houses

rank among Chinese folk houses. For example, the gate of even an ordinary quadrangle courtyard in Beijing was equivalent to the high-ranking "General's Gate" in the Suzhou area. This phenomenon is due to the fact that in Beijing, the capital city, officials were the main inhabitant of the quadrangle courtyards.

The standard quadrangle courtyard in Beijing is divided into two compounds, the inside compound and outside compound. A beautiful central gate was set up between the two compounds, and was often highly decorated. The gate inside is called screen door, consisting of six small doors, and it was opened only for the visit of distinguished guests. The everyday means of entry to the courtyard was through the left and right sides, avoiding the screen door after entering the first gate.

All the houses in the quadrangle courtyard in Beijing are bungalows without any storied buildings. The roof of the quadrangle courtyard was not to be higher than the stone platform base of the emperor's Hall of Imperial Throne. Seen from afar, the grandness and splendor of the imperial palace buildings on the central axes of Beijing made a clear contrast with the relatively low quadrangle courtyards and their swatches of grey rooftops, fully symbolizing the rulers' centrality and supremacy.

The plan of a community in Shaoxing, Zhejiang Province

Jiangnan Houses

The lively Jiangnan water village folk houses clearly differ from the imposing domestic architecture of the north. Jiangnan is a region in the lower Yangtze valley, including southern Jiangsu and northern Zhejiang provinces. The climate in the Jiangnan area is warm to hot, with plentiful rainfall and numerous natural rivers and lakes. It has long had a developed economy. To meet the requirements of transport, life and production, people dug out many canals and channels to connect natural rivers and form a large waterway transport network as dense as a spider web. The water "roads" passing through whole cities or villages, together with densely scattered ponds and lakes, have formed a "water village" landscape special to this area.

Commonly, a Jiangnan folk house faced the street in front and a waterway at back. The main means of transport were boats, so every

household needed a private wharf. This wharf was an extremely important part of the residence, where inhabitants could wash; buy vegetables, wood, rice, oil and salt from boat merchants; and dump dust and waste.

Houses in the area usually had a narrow door and deep entrance. This gave access to the limited riverbank space, with its vital waterways, to as many households as possible. With this narrow entry, the plot had to extend more deeply, to guarantee a sufficient residing area. The walls of this type of folk house were painted in white, contrasting strongly against the grey-tile rooftops. The roofs of the principal houses were generally higher than those of the wing houses. The roof surfaces were connected low and high, giving a strong sense of levels.

The space utilization of Jiangnan folk houses is ingenuous, providing

The waterfront residential buildings in Nanxun, Zhejiang Province

a strong aesthetic effect while exhibiting an extremely rational functional arrangement. For example, there were covers at the entrances of the ladders leading up and down stairs. The entrances were covered at the daytime, when not in use, thus expanding the floor space. In addition, the windowsills, which protrude deeply, could be used as porches. The walls on both sides were available to hang clothing. These features created a changeable and flexible utilization of space.

The courtyard houses of the wealthy in some parts of Suzhou in Jiangsu province, and Shaoxing in Zhejiang province were built using central axial symmetry, which is quite unusual for residences. Furthermore, they feature eaves galleries in front of every house and rear private gardens, a layout often used in official architecture, namely house in front and garden at the back. While many currently existing private gardens in Suzhou and Yangzhou were built in attachment to these residential houses, the houses themselves were not often preserved, as only the gardens were deemed to have tourist value.

Yan'an University in Shaanxi Province takes the architectural form of cliff-leaning caves.

Cave Houses

Most parts of Gansu, Ningxia, Shanxi, Shaanxi and Henan provinces are located on the ocher, or loess, plateau in northwest China, where the climate is dry and short of rainfall. The trees are sparsely scattered. Therefore, people living in these areas have traditionally used caves as dwellings, following local custom and saving on wood usage.

The folk cave houses are extremely practical. Warm in winter and cool in summer, they afford a comfortable and quiet interior. The architecture is solid and protective, and more earthquake-resistant than wooden houses. They last longer and do not require rebuilding of the roof every decade. It can be said that the folk cave houses are a perfect form of tailor-made residence.

Based on location and form, the caves roughly fall into three types: sunken caves, freestanding caves and cliff-leaning caves. The cliff-leaning

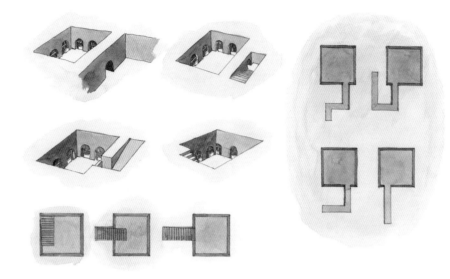

Diagrams and elevation showing the distribution and utilization of the interior space of sunken cave dwellings

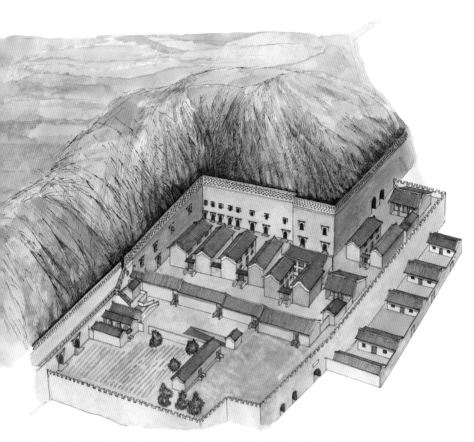

Kangbaiwan Manor in Gongyi is representative of civilian cave houses in Henan Province.

cave is built up against a mountain or hillside, with the open flat land in the front as the courtyard. This kind of cave takes full advantage of the material taken from the spot. The cost is low, but it can only be used where there are ravines or cliffs.

During its long period of use, people have rediscovered the advantages of the cave and adapted its architecture periodically. Initially people used caves to save resources and expenses, but with the improvement of economic conditions, people still wanted to have the advantages of underground caves, although they were willing to use more resources for them. Therefore, we have the freestanding cave. This cave built of bricks on flat land is the most expensive kind among the folk cave houses. The freestanding cave feels the same as the dug cave, but with more delicate exterior decoration. The folk houses in the Pingyao area of Shanxi are outstanding examples.

Most unique among the folk cave houses is the sunken cave. Among the three types of caves, the sunken cave is the most rare and precious, and is also the form disappearing most quickly. The sunken cave has a courtyard dug from the flat land downwards. Then several caves are dug extending out from this courtyard on four sides. Thus, seen from above, it appears as a square opening, although this is only the courtyard; the actual living is underground, saving a lot of ground space. Like above-ground courtyard houses, there are also principal and wing rooms to the sunken cave. The rooms opposite the principal living space are auxiliary ones such as the kitchen and livestock and storage areas.

While Chinese traditional architecture consists mostly of wood structures with large rooftops, the sunken cave breaks with this form. Such a rare residential form should be recognized and understood by more people around the world as a cultural heritage. However, since the total area that the sunken cave occupies is large and the government encourages building of new houses, the sunken cave has been disappearing quickly in recent years.

Tulou (Earth Building)

Wars were frequent in central China in ancient times. As a result, some people from the Han nationality in central China immigrated to the mountainous areas in southwestern Fujian Province to avoid the wars. They became known as the Hakkas. The Hakkas often found themselves in fierce conflict with the aboriginal inhabitants, vying for the land, and

The Umbrella Building in Gaoche Village, Hua'an County, Fujian Province

defending attacks from others at the same time. To survive, they had to build a residential form adaptable to the mountainous environment that also provided ample protection.

After generations of peaceful habitation and reproduction, there was sufficient population as well as relevant economic power to sustain a large residential mode known as the Tulou (Earth Building). The name comes from the fact that the walls of these multi-story large residential house were built of rammed earth.

The rammed earth walls of Tulou were built on a foundation of cobblestones. The walls of Tulou are all very solid. Other than walls made of yellow rammed earth, there were also even more solid walls made a composite of earth, sand, lime and other components. In addition, when the wall was rammed, bamboo chips were used as studs. The bottom of the wall is generally relatively thick. The thickness can reach 2.5 meters in some

Jingjiang Building in Zhangpu County, Fujian Province

parts, growing thinner gradually when going upwards so as to reduce the weight burden on the foundation. Walls made in such a manner are not only solid, but also tough enough to resist earthquakes.

Tulou in Fujian take many forms, including square Tulou, round Tulou and semi-moon Tulou. The round Tulou is the most charming, described as a "flying saucer fallen from the sky, mushroom growing out of the land." Additional round buildings were often built within the outer round building, thus forming circle after circle. For reasons of lighting and ventilation, the inside round building was usually half as high as the outside one, although there are also exceptions.

One such example is Jinjiang Building located in Zhangpu County of Fujian Province. The three-ring structure gets higher gradually progressing from the outside to the inside. The Umbrella Building, located in Yangzhujing village in Hua'an County of Zhangzhou city in Fujian, has only two rings, the inner higher than the outer. Its location on the top of the mountain makes it look like an umbrella, hence its name.

Round Tulou usually consists of one to three rings, while four rings are rare. In addition, a one-story bungalow is sometimes built around the round Tulou. This is called Loubao (surrounding building). It is built mainly to provide more rooms, and relieve the pressure of housing inside the main structure.

The internal residential form of the round Tulou starts from a circular center and extend outwards like the water ripples on the lake, circle after circle, looking very magnificent. At the centermost spot is the ancestral temple; next in order progressing outwards are the ancestral hall and surrounded porch. Members of the clan reside in the outermost ring. The individual rooms are the same in size, with an area of about ten square meters, and use common ladders, so that every household has almost no privacy.

While the building method of Fujian Tulou originated as self-defense, it is also a layout conducive to family and community cohesiveness. The offspring of the original immigrant ancestors live together, forming an independent society in co-existence.

Pile Dwellings

The southwestern parts of China that are home to many ethnic minorities are hot and rainy. To keep away from the wet ground, and make use of abundant natural resources, people adopted pile, or stilt-style, dwellings. These dwellings use bamboo or wood as vertical columns and horizontal beams to set up small structures. People live on the upper story while the lower story is used for livestock or storage. Pile dwellings have a history of over ten thousand years, and exist in large numbers even now in the mountainous villages of Guangxi, Hunan, Sichuan, Hubei, Guizhou and

A stilt-style, or pile, dwelling of the Dai nationality in Xishuangbanna in Yunnan Province

Yunnan. While some residents are Han Chinese, most belong to a minority group.

The pile dwellings are mostly built on a relatively high slope, occupying as little usable land as possible. To win more living space, they take full advantage of the natural landscape of the mountainous areas and create rich kinds of residential housing.

Pile dwellings possess other advantages that cannot be found in other forms of buildings. Firstly, they are completely of wood, which is easily obtainable in the heavily forested Southwest. They have large usable floor space. The dwelling is light with a foundation that has a good water filtration. This helps to reduce mudslide disaster. For example, bamboo buildings in Xishuangbanna in Yunnan are not only light in weight, but can allow floods to pass through without causing damage, due to the interspaces of the bamboo skin. If the flood is severe, the bamboo skin can be removed from the beam framework to reduce the resistance of the house to the

The frame structure of a stilt-style dwelling of the Dai nationality

rushing waters, so it is not swept away. Thanks to these advantages, this kind of ancient form remains in use.

People living in pile dwelling have maintained much of the ancient lifestyle. In Huotang culture, for example, the Huotang, or hearth located at the center of the sitting room, is an extremely important component. When guests come, everybody sits around Huotang. The Huotang is holy and the center of a family, where all important decisions are made. It is also practical, serving as a place to boil water and cook rice. The fire in the Huotang is inherited from ancestors and carried on from generation to generation, day by day, year by year, never ceasing.

APPENDICES

Location and Period of Construction of Existing Ancient Buildings

Building Name	Period of Construction	Location	Page
The Great Wall (Qin dynasty)	Built around 214 BC	Baotou, Inner Mongolia Autonomous Region	33
The Terracotta Warriors	Built in the period between 246 and 208 BC	Lintong District, Xi'an, Shaanxi Province	34
The White Horse Temple	Initial construction started in 68, but the existing building was built during the Ming and Qing dynasties.	Luoyang, Henan Province	39
Yungang Grottoes	Built in the period between 460 and 494	Wuzhou Mountain, in the west of Datong, Shanxi Province	40
Longmen Grottoes	Construction started around 494, and continued for more than 400 years	Luoyang, Henan Province	40
The Qian Tomb	Construction started in 684	Qian County, Shaanxi Province	48
The Great Hall of Nanchan Temple	Built in 782	Lijiazhuang Village, Wutai County, Shanxi Province	52
The Great Hall of Foguang Temple	Built in 857	Near the Dou Village of Wutai County, Shanxi Province	52
Dayan Pagoda of Ci'en Temple	Built in 652	Inside Ci'en Temple, Xi'an, Shaanxi Province	55
Guanyin (Goddess of Mercy) Cabinet of Dule Temple	Rebuilt in 984	Inside Dule Temple, Ji County, Tianjin	61
Huayan Temple	Rebuilt in 1140	Datong, Shanxi Province	63
Longxing Temple	Expanded in the Song dynasty in 971	Zhengding County, Shijiazhuang, Hebei Province	65
The Wood Pagoda in Ying County	Built in the Liao dynasty in 1056	Ying County, Shuozhou, Shanxi Province	66

Location and Period of Construction of Existing Ancient Buildings

Building Name	Period of Construction	Location	Page
Jin Ancestral Temple	Construction started in the Northern Wei dynasty and expanded during 1023 – 1032	At the foot of Xuanweng Mountain to the southwest of Taiyuan, Shanxi Province	68
Dadu Capital City	Construction started in 1267 and lasted 20 years	Beijing	73
White Pagoda of Miaoying Temple	Construction started in the Yuan dynasty in 1271	Inside Miaoying Temple, Xicheng District, Beijing	75
Yonglegong	Construction started in the Yuan dynasty in 1247	Ruicheng County, Shanxi Province	76
The Forbidden City	Built during 1406 – 1420	Dongcheng District, Beijing	80
Imperial Tombs of the Ming Dynasty	Construction started in the Ming dynasty in 1409	At the foot of Tianshou Mountain, Changping District, Beijing	87
The Temple of Heaven	Construction started in the Ming dynasty in 1420	Chongwen District, Beijing	91
Chengde Summer Resort	Construction started in the Qing dynasty in 1703	Chengde, Hebei Province	97
Summer Palace	Construction started in the Qing dynasty in 1750	Haidian District, Beijing	99
Old Summer Palace	Initial construction began in 1707	Haidian District, Beijing	99
The Eight Outlying Temples	Construction started in the Qing dynasty in 1711	Chengde, Hebei Province	104
The Potala Palace	Expanded in the Qing dynasty in 1645	On the Red Mountain to the northwest of Lhasa, Tibet Autonomous Region	111
Jichang Garden	Construction started in the Ming dynasty	Wuxi, Jiangsu Province	114
The Humble Administrator's Garden (Zhuozheng Garden)	Construction started in the Ming dynasty	Suzhou, Jiangsu Province	114

Location and Period of Construction of Existing Ancient Buildings

Building Name	Period of Construction	Location	Page
Ge Garden	Construction started in 1818	Yangzhou, Jiangsu Province	116
Shihu Garden	Built in 1885	Weifang, Shandong Province	118
Ke Garden	Built in the Qing dynasty in 1885	Dongguan, Guangdong Province	120
Yuyinshanfang Garden	Construction started in the Qing dynasty in 1867	Panyu, Guangdong Province	120
Qingdongling	Construction started in the Qing dynasty in 1663	Zunhua, Heibei Province	121
Qingxiling	Construction started in the Qing dynasty in 1730	Yi County, Hebei Province	121
Confucius Temples	Construction started in 478 BC	Qufu, Shandong Province	126
Guozijian	Construction started in the Yuan dynasty in 1306	Guozijian Street, Andingmennei, Beijing	129
Courtyard houses	Emerged as early as the Han dynasty according to today's research	Beijing, central Shanxi Province and Yunnan Province	132
Jiangnan houses	The initial style emerged around the Ming dynasty	Southern Jiangsu and northern Zhejiang provinces	138
Sunken Cave Houses	Most of the existing dwellings were built in the Qing dynasty	Primarily in the countryside of Sanmenxia, Henan Province and Pinglu County, Shaanxi Province	141
Tulou (Earth Building)	The earliest existing were built in the Ming dynasty, while many are from the Qing dynasty and later.	Primarily in the countryside of Zhangzhou and Longyan in the southwest of Fujian Province	144
Pile dwellings	The initial style emerged around the Tang dynasty in these areas	The mountainous villages of Guangxi, Hunan, Sichuan, Hubei, Guizhou and Yunnan provinces	147

Dynasties in Chinese History

Xia Dynasty	2070 BC – 1600 BC
Shang Dynasty	1600 BC – 1046 BC
Zhou Dynasty	1046 BC – 256 BC
Western Zhou Dynasty	1046 BC – 771 BC
Eastern Zhou Dynasty	770 BC – 256 BC
Spring and Autumn Period	770 BC – 476 BC
Warring States Period	475 BC – 221 BC
Qin Dynasty	221 BC – 206 BC
Han Dynasty	206 BC – 220 AD
Western Han Dynasty	206 BC – 25 AD
Eastern Han Dynasty	25 AD – 220 AD
Three Kingdoms	220 AD – 280 AD
Wei	220 AD – 265 AD
Shu Han	221 AD – 263 AD
Wu	222 AD – 280 AD
Jin Dynasty	265AD – 420AD
Western Jin Dynasty	265 AD – 316 AD
Eastern Jin Dynasty	317 AD – 420 AD
Northern and Southern Dynasties	420 AD – 589 AD
Southern Dynasties	420 AD – 589 AD
Northern Dynasties	439 AD – 581 AD
Sui Dynasty	581 AD – 618 AD
Tang Dynasty	618 AD – 907 AD
Five Dynasties and Ten States	907 AD – 960 AD
Five Dynasties	907 AD – 960 AD
Ten States	902 AD – 979 AD
Song Dynasty	960 AD – 1279
Northern Song Dynasty	960 AD – 1127
Southern Song Dynasty	1127 – 1279
Liao Dynasty	916 AD – 1125
Jin Dynasty	1115 – 1234
Xixia Dynasty	1038 – 1227
Yuan Dynasty	1279 – 1368
Ming Dynasty	1368 – 1644
Qing Dynasty	1644 – 1911

Index

Index

Index

Index

Index

Index